GEONOMICS INSTITUTE FOR INTERNATIONAL ECONOMIC
ADVANCEMENT SERIES
Michael P. Claudon, Series Editor


*Debt Disaster? Banks, Governments, and Multilaterals Confront the Crisis*
edited by John F. Weeks

*The Canada-U.S. Free Trade Agreement: Implications, Opportunities,
and Challenges*
edited by Daniel E. Nolle

# THE CANADA-U.S. FREE TRADE AGREEMENT
Implications, Opportunities, and Challenges

*Edited by*
DANIEL E. NOLLE

NEW YORK UNIVERSITY PRESS
New York and London

Library of Congress Cataloging-in-Publication Data

The Canada-U.S. Free Trade Agreement : implications, opportunities, and
challenges / edited by Daniel E. Nolle.
     p.   cm. — (Geonomics Institute for International Economic
Advancement series)
   Papers presented at a conference entitled Making the Most of the
Canada-U.S. Free Trade Agreement, held in Middlebury, Vt. 5/3-5/89,
under the auspices of the Geonomics Institute for International Economic
Advancement.
   ISBN 0-8147-5764-2
   1. Canada. Treaties, etc. United States, 1988 Jan. 2—Congresses.
2. Tariff—Law and legislation—United States—Congresses.   3. Free
trade—United States—Congresses.   4. Tariff—Law and legislation—
Canada—Congresses.   5. Free trade—Canada—Congresses.   I. Nolle,
Daniel E., 1950-      II. Geonomics Institute for International Economic
Advancement. III. Series.
KF6668.C321988A33   1990
341.7'543—dc20                                                                89-14027
                                                  CIP

# CONTENTS

# ACKNOWLEDGMENTS

This book grew out of the conference Making the Most of the Canada-U.S. Free Trade Agreement, May 3-5, 1989, in Middlebury, Vermont, under the auspices of the Geonomics Institute for International Economic Advancement. The inspiration for that event came from Michael P. Claudon, president of the Geonomics Institute, and I would like to thank him for giving me the opportunity to be a part of it. In addition, I very much appreciate his active and enthusiastic participation in a number of crucial phases of the development of the conference.

A good deal of the credit for the success of the conference belongs to the Geonomics staff, specifically Elizabeth Leeds, who worked tirelessly on issues large and small in coordinating the conference, all the while maintaining her friendly charm and good sense, and Events Coordinator Nancy Ward, who ably pinch-hit on several crucial occasions. In addition, a number of people were particularly gracious in giving of their time and advice. At a minimum, this group includes Jean Hennessey, Director of the Institute on Canada and the United States, Dartmouth College; Lucie Latulippe, Public Affairs, Québec Government Office; John Leehman, Vice President, Bread Loaf Construction Company; Robert Letovsky, Assistant Professor, Department of Business Administration, St. Michael's College; Kent Shaw, Editor, Geonomics Institute; David K. Smith, Professor Emeritus of Economics, Middlebury College; and Tim Soule, Director, Franklin County Industrial Development Corporation.

In preparing the manuscript, Colleen Duncan, Geonomics' Senior Editor, certainly deserves the huge measure of respect and thanks I gratefully accord her for overseeing the editorial process. Her good nature, competence, and professionalism made the process of producing this monograph a real pleasure. Thanks are also due to Editorial Consultant Elizabeth Leeds and Intern Lynn Ellis for their able assistance in production of this volume.

**Daniel E. Nolle**

# FOREWORD

Initiated in 1987 and finally ratified by both governments in 1989, the Canada-United States Free Trade Agreement (FTA) will result in the virtual elimination of impediments to the free flow of goods and services between these two intensively trading countries. To that end, it represents a bold step toward the eventual implementation of a North American free trade area, reaching from Mexico in the south to Canada in the north.

The FTA has five key provisions: (1) all tariffs on Canada-U.S. trade will be eliminated over ten years; (2) nontariff barriers to trade will be greatly reduced; (3) investment flows between the two countries are greatly liberalized; (4) impediments to cross-border business travel are eliminated or greatly lessened; and (5) impartial procedures for the resolution of trade disputes have been established.

Given the fact that the United States already purchases 75 percent of Canadian exports (20 percent of Canada's Gross Domestic Product), and that Canada is by far the largest recipient of U.S. exports, the FTA's potential benefits, especially for Canada, are striking. Consumers' real incomes will rise in both countries as resources are used more efficiently and manufacturers are able to reap productivity gains from larger-scale operations.

The transition to free trade will not be devoid of adjustment costs, however. Inefficient businesses in both countries will face new competition. Business failures will occur and jobs will be lost, but these costs are likely to be rather small when compared to the FTA's potential long-run benefits. For example, the ten-year phaseout will greatly ease the necessary pace of adjustment. Also, there is a striking similarity in the industries both countries afford the most pronounced protection: food and beverages, clothing, textiles, and tobacco. Therefore, both countries' producers will benefit from access to the other's market in areas in which the largest tariff cuts occur, a fact that should substantially ease adjustment costs.

Against this rather general (macro-level) backdrop, the Geonomics Institute sensed the need for a body of work aimed not at professional researchers, but at businesses on both sides of the border. What does the FTA mean for them? What new opportunities and challenges does it present? This book, which grows out of an exciting and at times provocative three-day conference convened in May 1989, answers these questions. It is operational, not abstract or theoretical, and provides a practical, nontechnical guide to help you learn how to get the most out of this historic agreement.

The Geonomics Institute seeks to promote a clearer and more complete understanding of international economic issues within and among the business, academic, and government communities. Geonomics is dedicated to sponsoring and publishing policy-oriented research. Annual conference series for North-South and East-West projects provide sustained forums for diverse groups of academic and business researchers and government representatives to examine, debate, and illuminate specific sets of issues. Geonomics is privately funded, nonpartisan, and not for profit.

We welcome ideas and opinions for better achieving our goals.

Michael P. Claudon
**President and Managing Director**
**Geonomics Institute**

# INTRODUCTION:
## The FTA's Implications, Opportunities, and Challenges—What Do We Look for Now?

*Daniel E. Nolle*

In the several years preceding the January 1989 implementation of the Canada-U.S. Free Trade Agreement (FTA), many worthy analyses of the economic effects for both countries and commentaries on the social implications for Canada appeared.[1] We can certainly expect much analysis and commentary on the impact of the FTA after the passage of several years, once observers have taken the time to track and ponder the effects of the agreement. This, of course, leaves a gap in our understanding of the implications of the FTA, one that is likely to be particularly troublesome to business leaders and policymakers on both sides of the border: What are the immediate effects, opportunities, and challenges of the newly implemented and vastly complicated agreement? It is the purpose of this book to help fill this gap.

This volume, like the conference from which it emerged,[2] is not intended to be a comprehensive assessment of the FTA to date. It is, however, intended to be timely. Authors of the papers included in this volume were asked, in effect, to respond to the question "Among the many aspects of the FTA, upon what, in the immediate aftermath of the agreement's implementation, is it important and useful for policymakers and business leaders to focus?" The answers given by this distinguished group of observers can be summarized as

---

1. See Jane Little's references at the end of Chapter 1 in this volume for an excellent list of analyses of the economic impact of the FTA. In addition to those references, Shea (1988) provides a comprehensive survey of the empirical literature estimating the economic effects of the FTA.

2. *Making the Most of the Canada-U.S. Free Trade Agreement,* sponsored by the Geonomics Institute, Middlebury, Vermont, May 3-5, 1989.

follows. First, some of the anticipated economic effects have already become evident, and based on this it is reasonably clear that one ought to focus on particular geographical regions on both sides of the border. This in turn points to a consideration of particular industries within selected regions, among which the energy sector is significant. Second, much of the immediate "action" surrounding the implementation of the FTA will focus on disputes, both new and long-standing. Hence, a review of the provisions in the agreement for dispute resolution, as well as an identification of several existing or likely sources of friction, is crucial. Finally, the question of the impact of the adoption of the FTA on Canadian cultural identity will continue to be "on the table." In light of this, all parties ought to develop as complete an understanding of this issue as possible.

In Part I of this volume, Economics and Energy, Jane S. Little points out that while the overall economic benefits for both the United States and Canada are likely to be modest, the effects of the agreement will vary considerably across regions. On the U.S. side of the border, the northern tier states, particularly New England, will be noticeably affected. Correspondingly, the province of Québec, with which the New England states trade most extensively, receives the most attention from all three papers in this section. Surveying the limited but suggestive post-implementation evidence, Little concludes that New England firms have begun to take advantage of the opportunities for increased trade.

In line with the regional perspective recommended by Little's analysis, William F. Averyt and Jean-Thomas Bernard focus attention on the energy sector, an extremely important area for both New England and Québec. At first blush, it would not seem necessary to analyze this industry. After all, much of the trade in energy between Canada and the United States, particularly trade in electricity, has been relatively unfettered for years; and, in a sense, electrical energy trade can be said to have served as a model for more liberalized trade between the two countries. In fact, though, Chapter Nine of the FTA focuses exclusively on "energy goods." Furthermore, as the Averyt paper in particular points out, the FTA significantly impacts energy trade inasmuch as the agreement is an additional rather large piece in a policy mosaic combining economic, regulatory, and environmental concerns.

The papers in Part II, Dispute Resolution Under the FTA, do not have a geographical focus; rather, their concern, in a number of respects, is with timeliness. Frank Stone's paper, which begins with a description of the historical roots of trade liberalization negotiations in general and dispute resolution in particular between Canada and the United States, also provides the reader with a comprehensible, useful explanation of the intricacies of Chapters Eighteen and Nineteen. William S. Merkin's paper moves from an explanation of FTA dispute resolution mechanisms to an identification of a number of current, or likely, disputes. This paper, by one of the chief U.S. negotiators,[3] is especially interesting for its suggestion that the settlement of existing disputes, let alone future disagreements, presents a serious challenge to parties on both sides of the border, notwithstanding the elaborate machinery incorporated in the FTA. Bearing this in mind, the final paper in the section by Jack R. Miller offers some hope that private-sector initiatives for dispute resolution not only are possible, but indeed can be viewed as a logical extension of the FTA provisions.

The two papers in Part III, Canadian Identity and the FTA, together provide a summary and an assessment of the rancorous debate in Canada over the extent to which Canadian cultural identity will be affected by the FTA. Both the paper by Peter Brimelow and that by Maureen A. Farrow and Robert C. York call attention to the fact that the FTA is an agreement on extending an *economic* relationship, not a political or social policy agenda. Furthermore, Brimelow points out that there is not a simple "for" and "against" dichotomy in Canada on the FTA. Rather, he argues that there are a number of quite distinct perspectives on the FTA and, indeed, on the issue of cultural identity, which break down along both ethnic and regional lines. Brimelow goes a very controversial step further by suggesting that it is even "entirely respectable" for some regions of Canada to actively seek to identify more closely with the United States. Farrow and York do not take this radical tack. Rather, they conclude that in the long run the benefits forthcoming from the implementation of the FTA will result in a stronger and more independent Canadian nation.

What do these papers teach us? First, we must look for the implications of the FTA, as well as the opportunities afforded by the agreement, at the "micro" level rather than the "macro" level. That is, our attention should be focused on differing regional and industry impacts and opportunities, or better, on the implications and opportunities for firms and individuals. Second, even to the extent we focus on the economic effects of the FTA, we must remember that these are intertwined with other ongoing events.

---

3. During the FTA negotiations, Merkin was the Deputy Chief U.S. Negotiator for the U.S.-Canada Free Trade Agreement as part of his duties as the Deputy Assistant U.S. Trade Representative for Canada, Office of the United States Trade Representative, a position from which he resigned in January 1989.

Third, the formal dispute resolution mechanisms, though the fruit of much intense negotiation, are receiving and will continue to receive stringent tests from the "real world," challenges that need to be approached with flexibility. Indeed, in view of the continuing and still highly emotional debate on the broader impact of the FTA on Canadian identity, "flexibility" could serve as a watchword for all constituencies.

Finally, it is clear that the FTA must be viewed as a living thing. Improperly employed or neglected it can wither and even die; used properly and judiciously interpreted it can flourish. At this point, much more depends on how business leaders and policymakers interpret and use the agreement than on the past considerable labors of the architects of the FTA.

## APPENDIX: OUTLINE AND PRINCIPAL PROVISIONS OF THE CANADA-U.S. FREE TRADE AGREEMENT[4]

PART ONE: OBJECTIVES AND SCOPE

**Chapter One: Objectives and Scope**
Article 101    Establishment of Free Trade Area
Article 102    Objectives
Article 103    Extent of Obligations
Article 104    Affirmation and Precedence
Article 105    National Treatment

**Chapter Two: General Definitions**
Article 201    General Application

PART TWO: TRADE IN GOODS

**Chapter Three: Rules of Origin for Goods**
Article 301    General Rules
Article 302    Transshipment
Article 303    Consultation and Revision
Article 304    Definitions

**Chapter Four: Border Measures**
Article 401    Tariff Elimination
Article 402    Rounding of Interim Rates
Article 403    Customs User Fees
Article 404    Drawback
Article 405    Waiver of Customs Duties
Article 406    Customs Administration
Article 407    Import and Export Restrictions
Article 408    Export Taxes
Article 409    Other Export Measures
Article 410    Definitions

**Chapter Five: National Treatment**
Article 501    Incorporation of GATT Rule
Article 502    Provincial and State Measures

**Chapter Six: Technical Standards**
Article 601    Scope
Article 602    Affirmation of GATT Agreement
Article 603    No Disguised Barriers to Trade

---

4. This section draws upon U.S.-Canada FTA (1988).

**Chapter Nineteen: Binational Dispute Settlement in Antidumping and Countervailing Duty Cases**

**PART SEVEN: OTHER PROVISIONS**

**Chapter Twenty: Other Provisions**

**PART EIGHT: FINAL PROVISIONS**

**Chapter Twenty-One: Final Provisions**

## PRINCIPAL PROVISIONS OF THE FTA

The FTA's provisions can be grouped into four main categories: trade in goods, trade in services, foreign investment, and dispute resolution.

### Trade in Goods

*Tariffs:* The FTA phases out all tariffs between the two nations over a ten-year period that began January 1, 1989.   Tariffs are classified into three groups: tariffs in the first group were eliminated on January 1, 1989; those in the second group will be phased out in five equal annual steps ending on January 1, 1994; those in the third group will be eliminated in ten equal annual steps ending in January 1999.

*Nontariff Barriers:*
- Quantitative Restrictions: The FTA specifies a timetable for phasing out almost all quotas, embargoes, and minimum price requirements.[5]
- Government Procurement Policies: The pact reduces the threshold value on open, competitive bidding from $171,000 (as per the GATT Government Procurement Code) to $25,000 for suppliers from either country.
- Sectoral Trade: The agreement sets out specific conditions for liberalized trade in energy, agriculture, wine and distilled spirits, and automotive goods.  In the latter case, the Auto Pact of 1965 remains essentially intact; duty remissions earned by third-country automakers manufacturing in Canada and exporting to the U.S. market ended on January 1, 1989.

*Rules of Origin and Duty Drawbacks:* The rules of origin in the agreement require that goods using inputs imported from third countries must have enough value added within Canada or the United States to allow them to be classified, when exported, under a different tariff classification than that under which the imported inputs originally entered.  Duty drawbacks and custom user fees will be eliminated entirely by January 1994.

---

5. Exceptions to this are the retention of the U.S. Jones Act requiring U.S. coastal shipping to be handled by U.S.-built ships, and the retention of restrictions on log exports from both countries.

### Trade in Services

*National Treatment*: National treatment (that is, nondiscrimination as between domestic and foreign suppliers) is accorded to most commercial services.

*Temporary Entry*: Restrictions are eased on temporary entry of professionals and some other services personnel.

*Financial Services*: U.S. bank subsidiaries in Canada are exempted from Canadian limits on foreign banks' market share, capital expansion, and asset growth. (Canadian bank subsidiaries in the United States did not face such restrictions prior to the enactment of the FTA.)

### Foreign Investment

*Screening Requirements*: Screening requirements are eliminated on the establishment by U.S. investors of new businesses in Canada. Canada can apply screening requirements on U.S. acquisitions of existing businesses in Canada only to those acquisitions of C$150 million or more.

*Other Restrictions*: National treatment is to be accorded by each country to the other's investors. Most restrictions on direct investment between the two nations are eliminated, including performance requirements and domestic content rules.

### Dispute Settlement

*Cabinet-Level Binational Trade Commission*: The Canada-U.S. Trade Commission will oversee the implementation of the agreement and participate in dispute resolution.

*Binational Panel*: Unresolved disputes are to be referred to a binational panel of experts. Many disputes are subject to binding arbitration; in other cases, either party may retaliate.

*Countervailing Duties and Antidumping Measures*: Separate procedures are set up to handle disputes involving countervailing duties and dumping.

*Financial Services*: Financial services disputes are to be handled by separate consultative mechanisms under the aegis of both finance ministries.

## REFERENCES

Shea, Brian F.    1988.    "The Canada-United States Free Trade Agreement: A Summary of Empirical Studies and an Industrial Profile of the Tariff Reductions." *Economic Discussion Paper 28.* U.S. Department of Labor, Bureau of International Labor Affairs (March).

U.S.-Canada Free Trade Agreement.    1988.    Washington, DC: U.S. Government Printing Office.

# I ECONOMICS AND ENERGY

Economic theory tells us that the gains flowing from liberalized trade include a more efficient allocation of resources, lower prices, greater variety, and a higher standard of living.  Indeed, these concepts, reinforced by reflection upon the disastrous consequences of the rising tide of protectionism, propelled the negotiation of the Canada-U.S. Free Trade Agreement (FTA).  The papers in this section focus on the evident and likely economic effects of the pact, giving special attention to the energy sector.

In Chapter 1, Jane S. Little briefly reviews the theory behind the sources of the gains from liberalized trade, and then summarizes the consensus among economists on the likely magnitude of the economic benefits from the FTA.  As she points out, the overall gains on both sides of the border are likely to be modest.  However, regional impacts will vary widely, particularly on the U.S. side of the border.  The northern-tier states, especially the New England states, which have long had a more extensive trading relationship with Canada than has the rest of the country, stand to be most affected. Analyses suggest the the positive effects over a broad range of industries will outweigh the negative effects for a narrower range of industries in New England.  Indeed, sighting admittedly limited evidence since the implementation of the agreement in January 1989, Little shows how a number of New England industries have begun to take advantage of the FTA.

Following on Little's suggestion that we should focus on specific regions and industries, Chapters 2 and 3 turn attention to energy trade, emphasizing Québec-U.S. Northeast trade.  The importance of bilateral trade in energy for both Canada and the United States is reflected in the fact that the FTA includes an entire chapter on energy (Chapter Nine). As William F. Averyt points out in Chapter 2, the FTA removes a number of previous restrictions, allowing a greater role for market forces in determining Canada-U.S. energy trade flows. Ironically, however, as Averyt explains, energy trade after the enactment of the FTA has become more complicated. This is partly the result of the increasing competition, fostered by the FTA, between hydroelectricity and other energy sources. In addition, rising demand for energy in both the United States and Canada, increasing environmental concerns, and probable lack of any substantial increase in the U.S. Northeast's supplies of it own generating capacity in the foreseeable future all add to the problem. As Averyt sees it, though the FTA likely will reduce a good deal of the uncertainty previously surrounding Canada-U.S. energy trade, the obstacles presented by the growing complexity of the post-FTA energy environment ought to be met by a more coherent binational policy to realize the potential for expanded energy trade.

In Chapter 3, Jean-Thomas Bernard focuses on trade in electricity, noting that, in particular, there has been a twenty-fold increase in the volume of electricity exported by Québec to the United States over the past decade. Based on estimates of persisting (though narrowing) price and cost differentials favorable to Québec vs. the U.S. Northeast, Bernard expects continued growth in this trade. Interestingly, he sees little short-run impact from the FTA on Québec electricity exports because, as he points out, free trade in electricity between Canada and the United States existed prior to the implementation of the pact. However, in the longer run, the FTA probably will have a positive impact on this trade. Bernard reasons that even though price and quantity restrictions do not now exist, the formal prohibition of them will enhance the ability and willingness of both parties to sign long-term sales contracts. Nevertheless, it is not clear that the full potential for electricity trade will be exploited, due to environmental and regulatory concerns, even in the face of continuing encouraging market signals and the reduction in uncertainty flowing from the implementation of the FTA. Thus, Bernard is far from sanguine about the abilities of parties on both sides of the border to fully take advantage of the opportunities in this arena.

# 1 THE ECONOMIC EFFECTS OF THE CANADA-U.S. FREE TRADE AGREEMENT

*Jane S. Little*

The Canada-U.S. Free Trade Agreement (FTA) eliminates all tariffs and removes or moderates a host of other barriers to the free flow of goods, services, and investment between the two countries over a ten-year period. Because the FTA has been in effect only a short while, the observations in this paper are—perforce—somewhat speculative. Accordingly, this paper describes the impact that economists *think* the FTA will have on business.

Most studies assessing the economic impact of the FTA conclude that both countries will achieve modest gains in welfare with minimal adjustment costs. The modest size of the gains and risks reflects the fact that almost three-quarters of U.S.-Canada trade is already duty free and that the remaining tariffs are on average fairly low. The trade-weighted average is 3.8 percent for Canada and 2.3 percent for the United States (see Table 1-1).

For the United States, the welfare gains resulting from the FTA are generally estimated to be less than 1 percent of GNP, while for Canada the gains may be roughly 2 percent of GNP. Canadians are expected to gain more—and risk more—because bilateral trade plays a much bigger role in the Canadian economy. Although Canada is the largest export market for the United States (the U.S. exports more than twice as much to Canada as to Japan, its second largest customer), Canada absorbs about one-quarter of U.S exports while depending on the United States for three-quarters of its export sales.

15

Exports represent only 10 percent of U.S. output but 30 percent of Canadian output. As a result, U.S. exports to Canada account for only 2 to 2.5 percent of our GNP, while Canadian exports to the United States account for 25 percent of the Canadian GNP. Obviously, the stakes are vastly greater for Canada.

Nevertheless, to conclude that Canada may reap larger welfare gains than the United States does not mean that U.S. firms will not benefit. U.S. foreign investment is a major force in the Canadian economy. Indeed, in some Canadian manufacturing industries, affiliates of U.S. firms account for one-half of industry shipments; thus, U.S. firms are a part of the Canadian economy and will clearly share in Canada's welfare gains.

Moreover, even though the prospective gains appear modest, not proceeding with the FTA would have represented a significant loss. First, had the FTA collapsed, the cycle of trade frictions and retaliation that led up to the free trade negotiations could well have begun again and with new vigor. Moreover, failure to proceed would have represented a real setback to multilateral trade liberalization and would have undermined U.S. and Canadian credibility in the GATT negotiations.

Economists have identified four sources of gains from the FTA: (1) comparative advantage, (2) economies of scale, (3) macroeconomic repercussions; and (4) increased investment stemming from reduced uncertainty. Comparative advantage is a source of gains because national production costs vary with differences in climate, endowments of raw materials, technological strength and so forth; thus, countries gain by exporting the goods they can produce relatively cheaply to pay for imports from countries that have comparative advantage in some other products. The free trade pact is expected to lead producers to expand output according to their comparative advantage rather than, as has been the case, to make production decisions based on existing trade barriers. A firm will no longer need to set up a cross-border plant just to avoid a tariff, for example. As a consequence, consumers on both sides of the border will enjoy lower-cost products.

Economies of scale also provide a source of gains from trade. When firms face fixed costs, it is advantageous to spread these expenses over greater output; thus, economies of scale, including those stemming from specialization and long production runs, provide important gains from trade beyond those resulting from comparative advantage. With economies of scale, trade always offers the *opportunity* for a simultaneous increase in the diversity of products available and in the scale at which each is produced, *if* firms

Table 1-1.  Comparison of Post-Tokyo Round
Canadian and U.S. Trade Barriers

| Industry | Canada | | United States | |
|---|---|---|---|---|
| | Tariff Rate (%) | NTBs (Tariff Equivalent) (%) | Tariff Rate (%) | NTBs (Tariff Equivalent) (%) |
| Agriculture | 2.2 | 11.9 | 2.2 | 6.9 |
| Forestry | 0.0 | 0.1 | 0.2 | 0.2 |
| Fishing & Trapping | 0.2 | 0.0 | 1.4 | 0.0 |
| Metal Mines | 0.1 | 0.0 | 0.2 | 0.0 |
| Mineral Fuels | 0.4 | 0.0 | 0.3 | 0.0 |
| Nonmetal Mines & Quarries | 0.5 | 0.0 | 0.1 | 0.4 |
| Food & Beverage | 4.2 | 9.0 | 3.5 | 8.5 |
| Tobacco Products | 16.0 | 0.0 | 10.1 | 0.6 |
| Rubber & Plastic Products | 8.9 | 0.0 | 8.4 | 0.4 |
| Leather Products | 12.0 | 4.2 | 7.9 | 0.0 |
| Textiles | 8.9 | 0.0 | 7.3 | 0.4 |
| Knitting Mills | 21.5 | 0.0 | 12.6 | 0.4 |
| Clothing | 17.2 | 0.0 | 10.7 | 0.4 |
| Wood Products | 2.7 | 0.0 | 1.4 | 12.9 |
| Furniture & Fixtures | 12.6 | 0.0 | 3.0 | 0.8 |
| Paper & Allied Products | 4.0 | 0.0 | 0.9 | 0.3 |
| Printing & Publishing | 1.4 | 0.8 | 0.5 | 0.2 |
| Primary Metals | 4.0 | 1.3 | 2.2 | 4.2 |
| Metal Fabricating | 6.8 | 0.9 | 3.2 | 1.0 |
| Machinery | 4.7 | 0.9 | 2.5 | 3.0 |
| Transportation & Equip. | 2.3 | 0.0 | 0.5 | 0.0 |
| Electrical Products | 6.1 | 0.9 | 3.7 | 0.1 |
| Nonmetallic Mineral Products | 3.4 | 0.0 | 2.9 | 0.0 |
| Petroleum & Coal Products | 0.5 | 0.0 | 0.4 | 0.0 |
| Chemicals & Chemical Products | 5.6 | 0.0 | 2.2 | 1.2 |
| Misc. Manufacturing | 6.2 | 0.9 | 3.5 | 0.2 |
| Weighted Average | 3.8 | 1.0 | 2.3 | 1.8 |

Note:   Summary figures are low in part because the remaining high tariffs do indeed deter trade and thus get little weight in the trade-weighted averages.

Source: Adapted from Magun, Rao, and Lodh (1987, 25 and 141-53), by Brown and Stern.

respond to that opportunity. With imperfect competition, however, there is no guarantee that firms will actually take advantage of these possibilities.

An important question, then, is how big are the still unexploited economies of scale? Protected by Canada's relatively high tariffs and thwarted by real and threatened U.S. trade barriers, many Canadian manufacturers have chosen to focus on the domestic market and supply the whole range of products in each industry. Accordingly, in many industries Canada has a lot of small plants producing too many products in short production runs. On the other hand, much Canada-U.S. trade is already barrier-free, and in some industries Canadian firms already have access to the entire North American market. Under current circumstances, then, Canadian gains from bilateral free trade probably amount to 1 to 2 percent of Canadian GNP, as already mentioned. Because the U.S. market is ten times the size of the Canadian market, unexploited economies of scale are presumably less plentiful here.

A third source of welfare gains from the Free Trade Agreement involves the macroeconomic repercussions. As trade barriers and consumer prices fall, real disposable income rises. If consumer spending increases, and the economy is operating at less than full employment, then the result should be an increase in real GNP, a gain that would reinforce the gains from the reallocation of resources according to comparative advantage and from economies of scale.

A final source of gains from trade is the reduction in previously encountered uncertainties such as large swings in national energy policies and the U.S. habit of broadening its definition of "counteravailable subsidy," the type of subsidy requiring the U.S. government to impose offsetting duties. Reducing these uncertainties should increase investment and result in additional gains in welfare.

If the gains from a free trade agreement largely depend on whether or not firms actually take advantage of possible economies of scale and specialization, it is no wonder that some producers and workers on both sides of the border are wary. After all, rationalization could imply the death of a number of firms. And it is probably not much comfort to the people involved to know that consumers generally should be better off because the scale of production has increased—somewhere else.

Naturally, then, most people are particularly concerned about the impact of the FTA on their own industry because the effect could be a lot greater than the modest gains expected overall. Nevertheless, studies generally suggest that the FTA's impact remains small for most industries on this side of the border. For instance, Brown and Stern (1986), who expect a significant reallocation of resources among industries as well as increased specialization and intra-industry trade, find that for the twenty-nine U.S. industries examined, only five—footwear, leather products, miscellaneous manufactures, iron and steel, and nonferrous metals (such as aluminum)—experienced a decline in output of as much as one-half of one percent. Nonferrous metals faced the worst outcome, with output estimated to fall 14 percent. The estimated gains were relatively small as well. U.S. output was expected to rise one-half of one percent or more in wood products, textiles, clothing, furniture, paper, chemicals, nonmetal mineral products, and electrical machinery. For the biggest gainers—textiles, paper, and electrical machinery—output was found to rise 4 percent, 3 percent, and 1 percent respectively.

Adjustments on the Canadian side of the border appear to be much greater. Brown and Stern see output gains of 150 percent for nonferrous metals and 29 percent for iron and steel. They expect output to be 14 to 35 percent lower than it would have been in the absence of the FTA for Canadian textiles, paper products, nonmetal mineral products, and electrical machinery.

Similarly, Wilson and Behrens (1988) looked at the seventeen U.S. industries (together accounting for half of U.S. GNP) that they thought would be most affected by the FTA. They designated only five industries—plywood, coal, uranium, nonfuel mining, and fisheries—as unfavorably affected by the FTA. Moreover, their study points out that the industries favorably affected by the FTA account for 43 percent of U.S. GNP while those unfavorably affected produce only 1 percent of GNP.

As indicated at the outset, it is still far too early to see much impact from the FTA—apart from an upsurge in curiosity and interest—at least on the U.S. side of the border. Indeed, the most heartening development to date is that U.S. and Canadian businesses have besieged their trade officials with requests to speed up the tariff reductions. In response to requests involving 2,000 items, the first meeting of the Canada-United States Trade Commission announced that the two countries will hasten some tariff reductions scheduled for 1994. Nevertheless, anecdotal evidence suggests that most of the more fundamental developments analysts expected the FTA to encourage are in fact beginning to occur:

Case 1:  Economists have suggested that the FTA should lead to lower prices for consumers. Example: On January 1, the Canadian tariff (8 percent) on motor bikes disappeared, and Canadian importers dropped the Harley-Davidsons by $1,000.

Case 2:  The FTA is supposed to broaden horizons and expand trade. Examples: Adage, a Massachusetts computer peripherals company, has so far concentrated its export efforts on Europe and Asia. Now, however, it is considering opening a sales office in Canada. A Toronto baked goods maker has added a bagel line that made no sense for the Canadian market alone, but the baker expects to export 60 percent of the output to the United States. Alcan and Reynolds (nonferrous metals, note!) have both announced expansions of their Canadian operations.

Case 3:  The FTA should encourage the rationalization of North American production. Examples: Two days after the Canadian election, Gillette announced plans to stop manufacturing in Canada, and Canadian labor leaders thought their worst fears were being confirmed. By contrast, the Canadian unit of Stanley Works expects to expand output and double its exports of tool boxes to the United States in five years. Canada has been hit by a virtual wave of acquisitions since the beginning of the year. The two largest Canadian glass concerns plan to merge and close duplicate plants. A spokesperson said that both companies had been making so many shapes, sizes, and colors that each had been operating at half speed. Similarly, Molson and Carling O'Keefe have merged and plan to eliminate seven of sixteen breweries, cut jobs, and double exports to the United States. More encouragingly, Novacor Chemicals of Alberta bought an Ontario polyethylene plant previously dedicated to the Canadian market. The plant will produce half as many products as before but in greater quantity and aimed, of course, at the U.S. market. Incidentally, Novacor's parent operates a gas pipeline network and expects to add conduits to the United States because the FTA ensures long-term access.

Case 4:  The FTA is expected to produce spillover effects. Example: Bankers, truckers, airlines, AT&T, and construction workers in the Detroit/Windsor area (where the port, bridge, and tunnel need upgrading) all expect to benefit from increased business resulting from the FTA.

Just as the Free Trade Agreement is expected to have an above-average impact on certain industries, it may also have an above-average impact on certain regions. New England is one of the areas for which the FTA is likely to be particularly important. First, New England is the most export-oriented region in the country. Within New England, Vermont, after Washington, is the second most export-oriented of the forty-eight contiguous states. Connecticut and Massachusetts are in fourth and fifth place. In addition, New England is more dependent on trade with Canada than is the country as a whole (see Table 1-2). New England does 30 percent of its trade with Canada (both imports and exports), while the country depends on Canada for a quarter of its exports and a fifth of its imports. Obviously, geography plays a role since the figures are even higher for Maine, New Hampshire, and Vermont. Equally obviously, removing trade barriers right in their own backyard should open some excellent opportunities for New England firms, especially those that are small, those that are in mature or niche industries, and those for which proximity is a factor. Although the Canadian market is one-tenth the size of the U.S. market, that is still a large market. If the U.S. market is only growing 1 percent a year, as in the case of apparel, say, then gaining access to the Canadian market represents a significant opportunity. Moreover, proximity often *is* a consideration. The widespread adoption of just-in-time inventory systems may recently have boosted its relevance, for instance, as may an increased emphasis on customized design and service within manufacturing from textiles to high-tech machine tools. A glance at the map suggests the particular importance of these factors for Northern Vermont. For centuries, the border has forced Vermont businesses to look south to rather distant markets in Boston and New York. Now they have direct access to Montréal, a vibrant city of 3 million people. That is a market three-quarters the size of Boston at roughly a third the distance.

Luckily, the U.S. industries that may be adversely affected by the FTA are not—with the exception of fisheries and footwear—prominent in New England. By contrast, the U.S. sectors expected to prosper under the FTA are well represented in the region—particularly electronics, of course, but also paper and, to a lesser extent, textiles. More generally, because New England specializes in sophisticated capital equipment, Canadian firms' efforts to rationalize and expand should benefit New England disproportionately.

New Englanders may also have an above-average tendency to engage in foreign investment. Though there is little evidence to support this conjecture, it is clear that such investment is usually linked with export activity and that the high-tech industries where foreign investment is prevalent are well represented in the region. A recent survey by the Bank of Boston (1989) provides a scrap of evidence here. A larger share of the New England firms responding to the survey had affiliates in Europe than did respondents from the Atlantic, the Southeast, or the Great Lakes, the other areas covered by the survey. Accordingly, New England firms are likely to find the FTA's provisions on national treatment of foreign investment particularly helpful—both as they relate to future Canadian investments and as they serve as a model for multilateral agreements. Moreover, should New Englanders really have an above-average proclivity for foreign investment, they should also have above-average opportunities for rationalization.

On this issue of foreign investment, the view from Vermont differs a bit from the view further south. Vermont sees itself as the recipient of inbound Canadian investment rather than as a source of outbound capital heading for Canada. Because Vermont is more dependent than most states on Canadian investment (Canadian firms account for 20 percent of employment at foreign-owned firms at the national level, but for 30 percent in Vermont), some Vermont residents are concerned that the Free Trade Agreement may have eliminated the *raison d'etre* for Canadian investment in the state. Indeed, some Canadian cross-border investment probably does reflect real or threatened U.S. trade barriers.

These worries may, however, be exaggerated since the FTA does not remove all motives for investing on this side of the border. For example, while the FTA prohibits discrimination in much federal procurement, buy-domestic policies persist at the state and local levels. In addition, multilateral operations help to diversify against various risks—from exchange-rate fluctuations to labor unrest. Indeed, observers suggest that occasional rumblings from Québec's strong unions and provincial politicians may continue to steer Québec investments toward Vermont. Most importantly, the FTA should add greatly to Vermont's attractions to non-Canadian investors, who, after all, account for 80 percent of the employment at foreign-owned firms. Without that border, Vermont's location looks much more centralized—less tucked away in a far corner of the country by itself.

There are conflicting assessments of the FTA's impact on energy trade. Nevertheless, the FTA's energy provisions, which prohibit

Table 1-2. New England and U.S. Merchandise
Exports to and Imports from Canada, 1987
(Millions of Dollars)

| | | Exports | | | Imports | |
| --- | --- | --- | --- | --- | --- | --- |
| | Total | To Canada | Canadian Share | Total | From Canada | Canadian Share |
| New England | 11,738 | 3,575 | 30.5% | 20,659 | 6,173 | 30.0% |
| Connecticut | 2,616 | 823 | 31.5 | 7,356 | 829 | 11.3 |
| Maine | 500 | 263 | 52.6 | 767 | 995 | 129.7[a] |
| Massachusetts | 6,967 | 1,774 | 25.5 | 10,026 | 2,706 | 27.0 |
| New Hampshire | 710 | 208 | 29.3 | 536 | 364 | 67.9 |
| Rhode Island | 383 | 139 | 36.3 | 1,175 | 245 | 20.9 |
| Vermont | 562 | 368 | 65.5 | 799 | 1,034 | 129.4[a] |
| United States | 252,866 | 59,814 | 23.7 | 405,901 | 71,085 | 17.5 |

a. Clearly, imports from Canada cannot exceed total state imports, and the two data sets used to construct this table are not consistent. In addition, allocating imports and exports by state is fraught with difficulties for U.S. and Canadian authorities. For example, the U.S. trade data by state include over $60 billion of both exports and imports that are "unallocated" for various reasons.

Sources: Statistics Canada (1987a, 1987b); U.S. Bureau of the Census (1987).

restrictions on the import and export of energy products (with limited exceptions), may be particularly valuable to energy-short New England, where a lack of adequate power could become a constraint on growth. Although some analysts have argued that the FTA's energy provisions merely codify current contractual practice, they do elevate such practice to the national policy level and should prevent a return to the blatantly discriminatory energy policies both countries have displayed from time to time in the past. Currently, inadequate transmission facilities pose a major obstacle to increased imports of Canadian gas and electricity. With access secured by treaty, investors should be more willing to build the required, very expensive infrastructure.

New England is also more service-oriented than the rest of the nation. Finance, insurance and real estate, and nonfinancial services both account for a larger share of employment in the region than in the nation at large. The region's manufacturing sector is even becoming service-oriented faster than the nation as a whole. While the production workers' share of manufacturing employment is declining everywhere, the trend is particularly pronounced in New England, where high-tech industries are placing increased emphasis on nonproduction activities such as research, design, sales, and after-sales service. Accordingly, the FTA's provisions concerning nondiscrimination in banking, insurance, and most commercial services, as well as its provision easing business travel, may prove particularly valuable to New England firms. Because the FTA is the first trade pact covering services and investment, both governments hope it will serve as a model in multilateral trade negotiations. If this model is adopted by the GATT, the benefits for New England will be multiplied.

Although the economic gains from the Free Trade Agreement may well be modest for both countries when viewed from a national perspective, the regional effects will vary widely. New England in particular stands to gain significantly; and, judging from the anecdotal evidence, a number of New England firms have already seized upon opportunities offered by the FTA. In addition, the successful implementation of the Free Trade Agreement is likely to enhance prospects for trade liberalization in other forums. If so, the positive effects of the FTA could, after all, be far from modest.

## REFERENCES


Baldwin, John R., and Paul K. Gorecki. 1983. *Trade, Tariffs and Relative Plant Scale in Canadian Manufacturing Industries: 1970-1979.* Discussion Paper 232. Ottawa: Economic Council of Canada.

——. 1985. "The Relationship between Trade and Tariff Patterns and the Efficiency of the Canadian Manufacturing Sector in the 1970s: A Summary." *Canada-United States Free Trade.* Ed. John Whalley with Roderick Hill. Toronto: University of Toronto Press, pp. 179-92.

Baldwin, John R., and Paul K. Gorecki, with J. McVey, and J. Crysdale. 1983. *Trade, Tariffs, Product Diversity and Length of Production Run in Canadian Manufacturing Industries: 1970-1979.* Discussion Paper 247. Ottawa: Economic Council of Canada.

Bank of Boston, Economics Department. 1989. "U.S. Manufacturing Firms' Attitudes Toward 1992." Boston, MA (February).

Beckman, Steve. 1988. "The United States-Canada 'Free Trade Agreement.'" Unpublished Analysis. Washington, DC: United Automobile Aerospace Agricultural Implement Workers of America (UAW).

Biggs, Margaret. 1987. "An International Perspective." *Perspectives on a U.S.-Canadian Free Trade Agreement.* Eds. Robert M. Stern, Philip H. Trezise, and John Whalley. Washington, DC: The Brookings Institution, pp. 129-54.

Brown, Drusilla K., and Robert M. Stern. 1986. "Evaluating the Impacts of U.S.-Canadian Free Trade: What Do the Multisector Trade Models Suggest?" Seminar Discussion Paper No. 171. Ann Arbor, MI: Department of Economics, University of Michigan (May).

——. 1987. "A Modeling Perspective." *Perspectives on a U.S.-Canadian Free Trade Agreement.* Eds. Robert M. Stern, Philip H. Trezise, and John Whalley. Washington, DC: The Brookings Institution, pp. 155-86.

——. 1988. "Computable General Equilibrium Estimates of the Gains from U.S.-Canadian Trade Liberalization." A paper presented at the Lehigh University Conference on Economic Aspects of Trading Arrangements. Bethlehem, PA (May 25-27).

Burgess, David F. 1987. "A Perspective on Foreign Direct Investment." *Perspectives on a U.S.-Canadian Free Trade Agreement.* Eds. Robert M. Stern, Philip H. Trezise, and John Whalley. Washington, DC: The Brookings Institution, pp. 191-215.

*Canada-U.S. Free Trade Agreement Synopsis.* 1987. Ottawa: International Trade Communications Group, Department of External Affairs.

Carmichael, Edward A.  1986.  *Confronting Global Challenges: Policy Review and Outlook, 1987.* Toronto: C.D. Howe Institute (December).

Corden, W. Max.  1987.  *Protection and Liberalization: A Review of Analytical Issues.* Occasional Paper 54.  Washington, DC: International Monetary Fund (August).

Cox, David, and Richard Harris.  1985.  "Trade Liberalization and Industrial Organization: Some Estimates for Canada." *Journal of Political Economy,* vol. 93 (February), pp. 115-45.

———.  1986.  "A Quantitative Assessment of the Economic Impact on Canada of Sectoral Free Trade with the United States." *Canadian Journal of Economics* (August), pp. 377-94.

Crandall, Robert W.  1987.  "A Sectoral Perspective: Steel." *Perspectives on a U.S.-Canadian Free Trade Agreement.* Eds. Robert M. Stern, Philip H. Trezise, and John Whalley.  Washington, DC: The Brookings Institution, pp. 231-43.

Daly, Michael J., and P. Someshwar Rao.  1986.  "Free Trade, Scale Economies and Productivity Growth in Canadian Manufacturing." *The Manchester School of Economic and Social Studies,* vol. 54 (December), pp. 391-402.

"Dismantling the 49th Parallel."  1987.  *The Economist.* (October 10), pp. 61-2.

"Farm Belt Grows Uneasy Over Canada-U.S. Free Trade."  1988.  *The Journal of Commerce* (January 19).

*The Financial Post 500.* 1987.  (May 18).

Frank, James.  1988.  "Adjusting to Free Trade: What Do the Numbers Tell Us?"  Ottawa: The Conference Board of Canada (March).

"A Free-Trade Milestone: The U.S.-Canada Pact is on a Scale with the EC."  1987.  *Business Week* (October 19), pp. 52-3.

Fuss, Melvyn, and Leonard Waverman.  1986.  "The Canada-U.S. Auto Pact of 1965: An Experiment in Selective Trade Liberalization."  NBER Working Paper No. 1953.  Cambridge, MA: National Bureau of Economic Research (June).

———.  1987.  "A Sectoral Perspective: Automobiles." *Perspectives on a U.S.-Canadian Free Trade Agreement.* Eds. Robert M. Stern, Philip H. Trezise, and John Whalley.  Washington, DC: The Brookings Institution, pp. 217-30.

Grey, Rodney de C.  1983.  "A Note on U.S. Trade Practices." *Trade Policy in the 1980s.* Ed. William R. Cline.  Washington, DC: Institute for International Economics, pp. 243-57.

Hamilton, Bob, and John Whalley.  1985.  "Geographically Discriminatory Trade Arrangements." *Review of Economics and Statistics,* vol. 67 (August), pp. 446-55.

Hearings Before the Subcommittee on Economic Stabilization of the Committee on Banking, Finance and Urban Affairs, House of Representatives, 99th Congress, Second Session. United States/Canada Economic Relations. Serial No. 99-97. 1987. Washington, DC: U.S. Government Printing Office (July 22, 31; August 5; September 11 and 23; and October 1, 1986).

Helpman, Elhanan, and Paul R. Krugman. 1985. *Market Structure and Foreign Trade: Increasing Returns, Imperfect Competition and the International Economy.* Cambridge, MA: MIT Press.

Henderson, Yolanda K., Richard W. Kopcke, George J. Houlihan, and Natalie J. Inman. 1988. "Planning for New England's Electricity Requirements." *New England Economic Review* (January/February), pp. 3-30.

Hill, Roderick, and John Whalley. 1985. "Canada-U.S. Free Trade: An Introduction." *Canada-United States Free Trade.* Toronto: University of Toronto Press, pp. 1-42.

Hufbauer, Gary Clyde, and Jeffrey J. Schott. 1985. *Trading for Growth: The Next Round of Trade Negotiations.* Policy Analyses in International Economics 11. Washington, DC: Institute For International Economics (September).

Lipsey, Richard G., and Murray G. Smith. 1985. *Taking the Initiative: Canada's Trade Options in a Turbulent World.* Observation No. 27. Toronto: C.D. Howe Institute.

Little, Jane Sneddon. 1988. "At Stake in the U.S.-Canada Free Trade Agreement: Modest Gains or a Significant Setback." *New England Economic Review* (May/June), pp. 3-20.

Magun, S., S. Rao, and B. Lodh. 1987. "Impact of Canada-U.S. Free Trade on the Canadian Economy." Economic Council of Canada Discussion Paper No. 331. Ottawa: Economic Council of Canada (August).

Magun, S., S. Rao, B. Lodh, L. Lavallée, and J. Peirce. 1988. "Open Borders: An Assessment of the Canada-U.S. Free Trade Agreement." Economic Council of Canada Discussion Paper No. 344. Ottawa: Economic Council of Canada (April).

Markusen, James R. 1984. "Multinationals, Multi-Plant Economies, and the Gains from Trade." *Journal of International Economics,* vol. 16 (May), pp. 205-26.

———. 1985. "Canadian Gains from Trade in the Presence of Scale Economies and Imperfect Competition." *Canada-United States Free Trade.* Ed. John Whalley with Roderick Hill. Toronto: University of Toronto Press, pp. 113-56.

Petri, Peter A. 1987. "Comments on a Modeling Perspective." *Perspectives on a U.S.-Canadian Free Trade Agreement.* Eds. Robert M.

Stern, Philip Trezise, and John Whalley. Washington, DC: The Brookings Institution, pp. 187-90.

Royal Commission on the Automobile Industry (The Bladen Commission). 1962. *Report.* Ottawa.

Royal Commission on the Economic Union and Development Prospects for Canada. 1985. *Report,* vol. 1. Ottawa: Minister of Supply and Services.

Rugman, Alan M. 1987. *Outward Bound: Canadian Direct Investment in the United States.* Canadian American Committee. Sponsored by the C.D. Howe Institute and the National Planning Association. Toronto and Washington, DC.

Rugman, Alan M., and John McIlveen. 1985. *Megafirms: Strategies for Canada's Multinationals.* Toronto: Methuen.

Schott, Jeffrey J. 1988. *United States-Canada Free Trade: An Evaluation of the Agreement.* Policy Analyses in International Economics 24. Washington, DC: Institute for International Economics (April).

Schott, Jeffrey J., and Murray G. Smith, eds. 1988. *The Canada-United States Free Trade Agreement: The Global Impact.* Washington, DC: Institute for International Economics.

Statistics Canada. 1987a. *Canadian Domestic Exports to Individual U.S. States, 1987, Customs Basis.* International Trade Division.

Statistics Canada. 1987b. *Canadian Imports from Individual U.S. States, 1987, Customs Basis.* International Trade Division.

Stern, Robert M., Philip H. Trezise, and John Whalley, eds. 1987. *Perspectives on a U.S.-Canadian Free Trade Agreement.* Washington, DC: The Brookings Institution.

Taylor, Teresa, and Matthew Berns. 1988. "The U.S.-Canada Free Trade Agreement: A Study of the Costs and Benefits to New England." A New England Council Report. Mimeo. Boston, MA: New England Council (March).

"They've Designed the Future, and It Might Just Work." 1988. *The Economist* (February 13), pp. 45-8.

Trezise, Philip H. 1988. "At Last, Free Trade with Canada?" *The Brookings Review* (Winter), pp. 16-23.

"UAW Board Votes Opposition to U.S.-Canada Trade Pact." 1988. *New from the UAW* (January 15).

United States General Accounting Office. 1986. *Report to the Chairman, Subcommittee on Oversight and Investigations, Committee on Energy and Commerce, House of Representatives, Canadian Power Imports: A Growing Source of U.S. Supply.* Washington, DC (April).

U.S. Bureau of the Census. 1987. *Highlights of U.S. Export and Import Trade,* FT990 (December).

"U.S.-Canada Free Trade Agreement: Summary of Major Provisions." 1987. Washington, DC: Office of Public Affairs, Office of the U.S. Trade Representative.

Whalley, John, with Roderick Hill, eds. 1985. *Canada-United States Free Trade.* Toronto: University of Toronto Press.

Wilson, Arlene, and Carl E. Behrens. 1988. *The Effect of the Canada-U.S. Free Trade Agreement on U.S. Industries: CRS Report for Congress.* Washington, DC: Congressional Research Service, Library of Congress (July 22).

Wonnacott, Paul. 1987a. *The United States and Canada: The Quest for Free Trade: An Examination of Selected Issues.* Washington, DC: Institute for International Economics (March).

———. 1987b. *U.S. and Canadian Auto Policies in a Changing World Environment.* Washington, DC: National Planning Association (July).

———. 1988. "Autos Strain Ties with Canada." *The Journal of Commerce* (February 11).

Yeutter, Hon. Clayton, U.S. Trade Representative. 1987. "Statement on Release of U.S.-Canada Free Trade Agreement Text" (December 11).

# 2 THE TRANSBORDER REGULATORY ENVIRONMENT FOR CANADA-U.S. ENERGY TRADE

*William F. Averyt*

The Canada-U.S. Free Trade Agreement (FTA) has rearranged not only the legalities of trade and investment across the Canada-U.S. border, but will also restructure the broader legal and political environment within which the legal rules operate. The very structure of forces shaping public policy between our two countries will change as a consequence of the operation of the FTA. This paper first sketches a "before and after" picture of the Canada-U.S. energy trade regulatory environment, giving special attention to Canada-New England energy ties. This is followed by a consideration of a number of important questions concerning future Canada-U.S. energy trade.

## ENERGY POLICY BEFORE AND AFTER THE FTA

Although most attention has been focused on the tariff elimination and investment policy aspects of the FTA, the energy chapter is one of the most important parts of the pact. The key aspects of the FTA include the following: minimum export prices may not be required; taxes and duties exclusively on energy exports may not be required;

31

and Canada may, in time of national emergency or shortage, reduce its energy exports to the United States only in direct proportion to the reductions made in its shipments to its own citizens (FTA 1988, 141-50). The purpose of these rules is to permit bilateral energy trade to be market-driven to the greatest extent possible.

Substantial liberalization has now occurred in North American energy markets because of the FTA, as well as earlier deregulatory steps within the Canadian and American domestic markets. However, the new configuration of market forces in certain regions, including the U.S. Northeast, is opening a new round of discussion and debate on the appropriate public policies for energy development in the 1990s.

Figure 2-1 provides a simple sketch of transborder regulatory forces operating before 1989. A Canadian hydro would sell to an American buyer following approval of the relevant state regulatory body. The various forces operating on this transaction are presented for both Canada and the United States. The major access point for the seller was the National Energy Board (NEB). By statute, the NEB issued export licenses after three criteria had been met to its satisfaction: (1) the export had to be priced to recover its "appropriate share of the costs incurred in Canada," (2) it could not be priced "less than equivalent service to Canadians in related areas," and (3) it had to be priced almost at the level of the least-cost alternative to the American buyer.[1]

For Hydro-Québec, the Canadian seller of most interest historically to New England, no provincial equivalent to the NEB existed (unlike, for example, the Albertan case). The major constraints on Hydro-Québec's operations, domestic or export, were and are more to be found in the overtly political realm. These constraints are in the form of the extent and speed of future development of hydro resources within Québec; and in the past two years significant differences of opinion have arisen between the Crown Corporation and the government on this issue. In late 1988, the Québec Ministry of Energy and Resources released its energy policy statement for the 1990s, commenting: "For its part, the government wishes to further strengthen investments in the development of hydroelectric resources, in particular through export sales higher than actually contemplated in Hydro-Québec's scenario" (1988).

---

1. Canada National Energy Board Act, Regulations, Part VI, c. 1056, 3(z).

**Figure 2-1.** Transborder Regulatory Environment (Pre-1989)

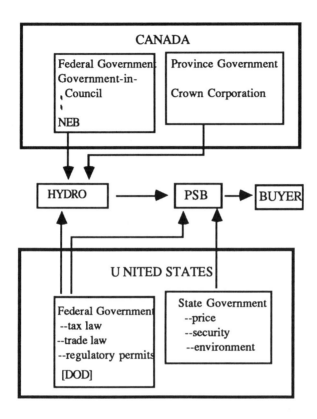

On the U.S. side, very few policy constraints existed. The Department of Defense reviewed the impact on American security of the physical construction of new transmission lines across the border, but no regulatory approval was necessary on the federal level for electricity imports. In fact, electricity did not even have a tariff number in the American tariff schedule before 1988, and certain Canadian officials argued that it could not be considered a traded good.[2] Within individual states, public service boards considered each contract, but the level of public debate was not rancorous.

Turning to the post-FTA environment, life becomes more complicated, but only in part due to the enactment of the FTA. Developments in the energy field and in the regulatory stance of various state public utility commissions in recent years have also greatly contributed to the complications illustrated in Figure 2-2. Of particular note is the impending head-to-head competition between hydroelectricity and natural gas, two energy forms that one Québec analyst has referred to as *les frères ennemis*, "enemy brothers."

The "interface" of competition between these two energy forms will be the increasing importance of the Independent Power Producers (IPPs) and their use of natural gas in cogeneration projects that produce heat and electricity. In essence, hydro exporters such as Hydro-Québec will be competing for future markets with IPPs using Canadian natural gas. The policy dilemmas facing the Québec government in future years will be especially interesting, since it has Crown Corporations selling both hydro power (Hydro-Québec) and controlling the major natural gas utility in the province (Gaz Métropolitain).

The range of forces and actors becomes quite large in the post-FTA environment. In New England, for example, transactions may be influenced on the gas side by the provinces of Alberta, Québec, and the Canadian federal government. It is worth pointing out here that the FTA basically removes the power of the NEB to restrict exports, shifting it instead to the Canadian government (the Prime Minister and his cabinet). In particular, the NEB must request government approval of a restriction. If the government refuses the request or does not answer the request, no restriction may be ordered by the NEB. Thus, the NEB's autonomous, quasi-judicial status has ended. Especially with regard to electricity exports, the NEB can no longer apply the so-called Third Price Criterion

---

2. U.S. Energy Information Administration (1986); and "Power for Export," *Maclean's*, December 15, 1986, p. 12. The tariff number in the new Harmonized System is 2716.00.00.00.

**Figure 2-2.** Transborder Regulatory Environment (Post-1989)

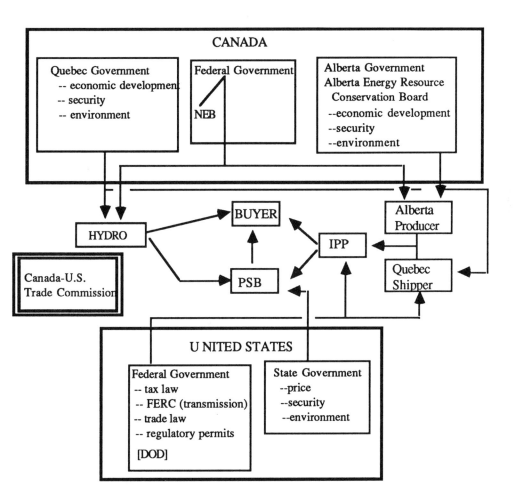

requiring the export price to be almost as high as the least-cost alternative to the American buyer (FTA 1987, Annex 905.2, p. 150). On the U.S. side, the policy environment has become much more complex also. The federal and state regulatory developments spurring the growth of gas-using IPPs and the federal tax treatment making such growth attractive (fast write-offs and investment tax credits) have a direct impact on the policy decisions of the states. In addition, as IPPs become more important players in the energy market, the question of transmission policy and the future role of the Federal Energy Regulatory Commission becomes more important.

## FUTURE DEVELOPMENTS OF CANADA-U.S. ENERGY TIES

This section raises a few questions about the post-FTA policy environment, based on current guesstimates of the nature of North American energy markets in the 1990s. The first question that comes to mind is the impact on Canadian energy development of the fierce competition arising among energy sources in the United States. Does this growing competition inside the U.S. market mean, for example, "no more Limestones"? (that is, hydros must sell before they build?) More specifically, are we beginning to see the signs of a Canadian policy debate in which Phase II of James Bay is pitted against the Mackenzie River delta, in which economic development goals of Québec are weighed against those of Alberta? Who will do the weighing? Recent past history of energy production, development, and restriction policies in Canada shows how extremely powerful various provincial interests are and how difficult it is for the Canadian federal government to strike a national balance (Anderson 1985; Wilkinson 1984).

A second issue concerns the impact of the proportionality principle. The more export contracts that Canada approves, the larger the amount of energy exports protected by the proportionality clause. Every approved Canadian export contract gives Americans a legal claim on future Canadian energy production,[3] which was the bone of contention in the energy part of the tumultuous free trade debate in Canada last year.

---

3. See, for example, the discussion of the provision by Canadian Sen. Mitchell Sharp before the Canadian Senate Select Committee on Foreign Affairs, December 29, 1988, pp. 3:9-11.

A third concern involves the development of Canadian energy resources primarily to meet the growing U.S. demand. For example, a debate has arisen over the desirability of dedicating a large portion of Canadian Arctic Natural gas supplies to the American market. In this respect, the NEB decision on the pending application of ESSO Resources and Shell Canada to export 6 trillion cubic feet of gas from the Mackenzie River delta to the United States will be a critical bellwether.[4]

Greater overall U.S. demand for energy from Canada has also raised fears about adverse environmental effects. For example, the environmental impact of Phase II of the James Bay hydro development is being hotly debated in Québec. In addition, there are concerns about the impact of this project on the culture of the Cree Indians.

A final question to consider concerns the entry of new elements on the demand side of the energy equation. Here, the province of Ontario must be examined very carefully. Already, Ontario Hydro has indicated that it might be a competitor with New England for future electricity offerings by other Canadian hydros.[5] Ontario has also voiced its interest in the massive Esso-Shell proposal and has said that it may shift toward opposing the project if it appears that future gas supplies to this heavily populated central province are endangered.[6]

## CONCLUSION

It is clear that the policy environment for Canada-U.S. energy trade under the Free Trade Agreement has become much more complex. At first glance, this is surprising. The principal purpose of the FTA was to liberate trade as much as possible from government interference and pressures. Nevertheless, upon further considera-tion, the possibility of the policy environment becoming more complex seems likely due to the fact that we now have two national markets coming much closer together, and a certain amount of policy coordination friction is to be expected.

Another source of policy complexity, however, stems from the very deregulation under way in each national market. In the

4. See, for example, "Unfettered Sale of Northern Gas to U.S. Questioned," *Calgary Herald*, February 5, 1989, p. A7.
5. Remarks of Michael Spence, Conference on Canadian Hydro Exports, University of Vermont, April 28, 1989.
6. *Canadian Press*, March 13, 1989.

United States, for example, the competitive activity and uncertainty in the electric utility market is spilling over into the Canadian suppliers' market. The policy complexity results in large part from this spillover.

The challenge now facing both countries is to incorporate all of these elements into a broader, more coherent policy process that will evolve into a transborder process. This task will not be easy, but it should ultimately benefit all parties.

## REFERENCES

Anderson, F. J. 1985. *Natural Resources in Canada.* Toronto: Methuen, pp. 180-99.

Ministry of Energy and Resources. 1988. *Energy: Driving Force of Economic Development; Energy Policy for the 1990s.* Québec, p. 46.

*U.S.-Canada Free Trade Agreement.* 1988. Washington, DC: U.S Government Printing Office.

U.S. Energy Information Administration. 1986. *U.S. International Electricity Trade.* Washington, DC, p. 7.

Wilkinson, B. W. 1984. "Energy Revenue Sharing." *Canada's Energy Policy, 1985 and Beyond.* Eds. Edward A. Carmichael and Corina M. Herrera. Toronto: C.D. Howe Institute, pp. 59-69.

# 3 MARKET INDICATORS AND QUÉBEC-U.S. ELECTRICITY TRADE

*Jean-Thomas Bernard*

The rising significance to Québec of electricity trade is reflected both in statistics on the growth and volatility of exports to the United States and in the importance attached to recent policy initiatives. Electricity exports from the province of Québec to the United States rose from 0.6 TWh in 1977 to 16.4 TWh in 1987 and then dropped to 11.8 TWh in 1988.[1] Furthermore, the premier of Québec, Robert Bourassa, has put forward an economic development policy relying in part on building new hydro power plants to serve the export market.[2] This paper outlines the factors responsible for the past growth in Québec electricity exports to the United States and examines likely prospects for the future.

The increase of Québec electricity exports to neighboring American states came in response to such basic economic incentives as price and cost differentials between the two areas. Although it appears that these differentials will persist for a number of years,

Thanks are due to Danny Bélanger and James Roberts for their able assistance. This paper represents my views as an individual, and the usual disclaimer about responsibility applies.

1. The abbreviations used throughout this paper for measures of the volume of electricity are as follows: TWh = terawatt hours; MW = megawatt; and KWh = kilowatt hours.

2. See Bourassa (1985). This has been translated into official government policy in Government of Québec, Department of Energy and Resources (1988).

they will likely become smaller due to two main factors: (1) the increasing cost of bringing new hydro power sites on stream in the province of Québec, and (2) the competition from other sources of supply, including energy conservation, in the U.S. Northeast.[3] Furthermore, despite the potential for mutually beneficial trade, realized trade may fall short of this ideal potential. Electricity markets, because of the high degree of their public visibility, are subject to influences from a wide array of sources: regulators, government legislators, public utilities, special interest groups, and other private parties. Pressure from specific groups may add to costs so that basic economic incentives such as prices and production costs are not strong enough to be the main determinants of realized trade. Forces of this sort are at work both in Canada and the United States.

This paper takes the following structure. First, a brief survey is presented of the recent evolution of energy markets in the U.S. Northeast and in the province of Québec. Second, the main market indicators (prices and costs in the two regions) are examined to determine the likely prospects for future electricity exports. Third, the present state of Canadian electricity export regulations is considered, including an examination of the likely impact of the Canada-U.S. Free Trade Agreement (FTA) on electricity export regulations. Finally, there is a brief discussion of a number of policy issues concerning electricity trade on both sides of the Canada-U.S. border.

## ENERGY MARKETS IN THE U.S. NORTHEAST AND IN THE PROVINCE OF QUÉBEC, 1976-1986

To assess the evolution of the electricity market in the regions of interest, it is useful to have in mind its place within the overall energy market as well as the interrelationships among major energy sources.

### New England

Table 3-1 presents data on New England energy consumption by source from 1976 to 1986. The salient points of the table are the following:

3. The U.S. Northeast comprises the member states of the Northeast Power Coordinating Council (NPCC), that is, New York and the New England states.

**Table 3-1.** New England Energy Consumption Estimates by Source
(Trillions of BTU)

| Year | Coal | Natural Gas | Petroleum | Nuclear | Hydro | Other | Net Exchanges | Total |
|------|------|-------------|-----------|---------|-------|-------|---------------|-------|
|      |      |             |           | —————Electricity————— | | | | |
| 1976 | 27.2 | 258.3 | 2419.3 | 278.2 | 93.2 | 0.0 | -7.1 | 3069.1 |
| 1981 | 56.0 | 313.2 | 1778.1 | 284.5 | 95.1 | 0.3 | 69.3 | 2596.5 |
| 1986 | 156.8 | 317.7 | 1856.6 | 317.6 | 157.1 | 0.9 | 32.4 | 2839.1 |
| **Average Annual Growth Rates (%)** | | | | | | | | |
| 1976-81 | 15.5 | 3.9 | -6.0 | | | 4.3 | | -3.3 |
| 1981-86 | 22.9 | 0.3 | 0.9 | | | 2.5 | | 1.8 |
| **Shares (%)** | | | | | | | | |
| 1976 | 0.9 | 8.4 | 78.8 | | | 11.9 | | 100.0 |
| 1981 | 2.2 | 12.1 | 68.5 | | | 17.3 | | 100.0 |
| 1986 | 5.5 | 11.2 | 65.4 | | | 17.9 | | 100.0 |

*Source:* U.S. Department of Energy (1988b).

1. Total energy consumption decreased from 1976 to 1981 (-3.3 percent annually) and then increased from 1981 to 1986 (+1.8 percent).
2. Petroleum consumption declined at the rate of 6.0 percent in the first sub-period and posted a small increase (0.9 percent) in the second.
3. The three other energy sources, which compete with petroleum and also among themselves, displayed positive growth over the whole period. Except for coal, their growth was at a lower rate in the second sub-period.
4. Petroleum is still by far the single largest energy source due to its unique role in the transport sector.
5. Coal and electricity have benefited the most from the relative decline of petroleum.

A major drawback of the data shown in Table 3-1 is their failure to reveal the role played by coal, natural gas, and petroleum in electricity generation. This information appears in Table 3-2. After a period of almost no growth from 1976 to 1981, electricity generation by public utilities increased at the annual rate of 3.4 percent from 1981 to 1986. As inputs for electricity generation, coal and natural gas grew at particularly impressive rates over the whole period; natural gas, however, still makes a modest contribution to electric power generation. The use of petroleum by electric utilities declined steadily from 1976 to 1986, with its share among all inputs dropping from 54.4 percent to 38.6 percent. Coal took up most of the slack from the reduction of petroleum use. Nuclear, hydro, and other generating sources made relatively modest gains. While the New England states changed from being net exporters of electricity in 1976 to net importers in 1981 and 1986, net exchanges were still a relatively small part (3.1 percent) of total generation in 1986.[4]

Table 3-3 shows New England Power Pool (NEPOOL) installed generating capacity by source in 1988 as well as the forecast to the year 2000. Petroleum thermal plants provide the largest capacity share and are expected to maintain this leading position. In 1987, the petroleum-based units made up 47.3 percent of total New England capacity but generated only 37.3 percent of total electricity (U.S. Department of Energy 1988a).[5] This indicates that petroleum generating units are either peaking or are intermediate units under the load duration curve, while coal and nuclear units are

4. This is a net figure; it does not follow that gross flows are so small.
5. Almost all public utilities in New England are members of NEPOOL.

Table 3-2. Estimates of Energy Input to New England Electric Utilities
(Trillions of BTU)

| Year | Coal | Natural Gas | Petroleum | Nuclear | Hydro | Other | Total |
|---|---|---|---|---|---|---|---|
|  |  |  |  | ——Electricity—— | | | |
| 1976 | 20.7 | 3.8 | 455.2 | 278.2 | 79.2 | 0.0 | 837.1 |
| 1981 | 46.5 | 9.9 | 428.0 | 284.5 | 81.9 | 0.3 | 851.1 |
| 1986 | 140.2 | 16.1 | 389.2 | 317.6 | 144.0 | 0.9 | 1008.0 |
| **Average Annual Growth Rates (%)** | | | | | | | |
| 1976-81 | 17.6 | 21.1 | -1.2 |  | 0.5 |  | 0.3 |
| 1981-86 | 24.7 | 10.2 | -1.9 |  | 4.8 |  | 3.4 |
| **Shares (%)** | | | | | | | |
| 1976 | 2.5 | 0.5 | 54.4 |  | 42.7 |  | 100.0 |
| 1981 | 5.5 | 1.2 | 50.3 |  | 43.1 |  | 100.0 |
| 1986 | 13.9 | 1.6 | 38.6 |  | 45.9 |  | 100.0 |

Source: U.S. Department of Energy (1988b).

contributing base power. A striking feature of Table 3-3 is that despite the strong electricity demand growth experienced in the 1980s, generating capacity is forecasted to grow only slightly to the year 2000.

### New York State

Table 3-4 shows the data with respect to energy consumption by source in New York from 1976 to 1986. It can be seen that total energy consumption declined during the period. Electricity is the only energy source to show positive growth over the ten years; all other energy sources, with the exception of natural gas in the first sub-period, decreased. Petroleum is still the single most important source, although its share fell from 66.1 percent in 1976 to 50.3 percent in 1986, with natural gas and electricity filling the gap.

Table 3-5 presents energy inputs to New York electric public utilities. Total generation posted a modest increase over the whole period due to the strong showing by natural gas from 1976 to 1981 and to the steady growth of hydro and nuclear power. Petroleum inputs decreased rapidly with its share from 45.8 percent in 1976 to 25.1 percent in 1986.

Table 3-6 presents data on New York Power Pool generating capacity by source in 1988, as well as the forecast to the year 2000. Total generating capacity is seen to increase by 4,347 MW between 1988 and 1995, with little growth afterwards. Most of the near-term capacity growth is expected to be provided by nuclear (809 MW), purchases from non-utility generators (2,238 MW), and imports from Québec (500 MW).[6] Petroleum and coal are not expected to make any additional contribution, and hydro will register only a small increase.

### The Province of Québec

Table 3-7 shows the evolution of available energy by source in the province of Québec from 1976 to 1986. Total available energy declined continuously from 1976 to 1986 due to the decline in petroleum consumption, a factor that was particularly strong from 1981 to 1986. Both natural gas and electricity grew significantly,

---

6. Another 500 MW will be added in 1996 following a contract signed with Hydro-Québec on April 28, 1989.

Table 3-3. Forecasted NEPOOL Generating Capacity (Winter)[a]
M W

| Year | Nuclear | Coal | Petroleum | Hydro | Other[b] | Total |
|------|---------|------|-----------|-------|----------|-------|
| 1988[c] | 4819 | 2778 | 11091 | 3000 | 2551 | 24239 |
|       | (19.9) | (11.5) | (45.8) | (12.4) | (10.5) | (100.0) |
| 1990 | 6639 | 2778 | 11108 | 3125 | 3770 | 27420 |
|      | (24.2) | (10.1) | (40.5) | (11.4) | (13.7) | (100.0) |
| 1995 | 6639 | 2778 | 10426 | 3125 | 3153 | 26121 |
|      | (25.4) | (10.6) | (39.9) | (12.0) | (12.1) | (100.0) |
| 2000 | 6639 | 2654 | 10237 | 3125 | 2878 | 25533 |
|      | (26.0) | (10.4) | (40.1) | (12.2) | (11.3) | (100.0) |

a. December figures. Figures in parentheses are percentage.
b. Other includes wood, natural gas, purchases from independent producers and other electric public utilities, and imports.
c. Actual figures.

Source: NEPOOL (1989, 3).

with electricity increasing its share from 20.9 percent in 1976 to 38.6 percent in 1986. Electricity demand growth has been particularly strong in recent years, with regular electricity sales (excluding interruptible sales) going from 91.0 TWh in 1984 to 119.8 TWh in 1988, representing an annual growth rate of 7.1 percent. Over the same period, interruptible electricity sales in Québec decreased slightly from 9.9 TWh to 8.7 TWh. This impressive growth is not expected to last, and Hydro-Québec (1989) is forecasting that electricity demand in the province will grow at 2.7 percent per year to 2001. To satisfy the forecasted demand as well as the export market, Hydro-Québec is planning to add 11,161 MW of hydro generating capacity before 2001, which will be added to the 30,032 MW that were available on December 1, 1988.[7]

7. This consists of 22,836 MW (hydro), 5,443 MW (imports), 685 MW (nuclear), 600 MW (petroleum), 468 MW (other oil fired).

Table 3-4. New York Energy Consumption Estimates by Source
(Trillions of BTU)

| Year | Coal | Natural Gas | Petroleum | Electricity | | | | Total |
|------|------|-------------|-----------|---------|-------|-------|---------------|-------|
| | | | | Nuclear | Hydro | Other | Net Exchanges | |
| 1976 | 363.8 | 604.3 | 2763.0 | 173.0 | 324.4 | 0.0 | -50.5 | 4178.0 |
| 1981 | 308.7 | 775.7 | 1938.2 | 192.4 | 418.1 | 0.0 | -54.8 | 3578.3 |
| 1986 | 253.3 | 749.9 | 1710.1 | 238.7 | 466.2 | 0.0 | -21.1 | 3397.1 |
| **Average Annual Growth Rates (%)** | | | | | | | | |
| 1976-81 | -3.2 | 5.1 | -6.8 | | | 4.5 | | -3.1 |
| 1981-86 | -3.9 | -0.7 | -2.5 | | | 4.2 | | -1.0 |
| **Shares (%)** | | | | | | | | |
| 1976 | 8.7 | 14.5 | 66.1 | | | 10.7 | | 100.0 |
| 1981 | 8.6 | 21.7 | 54.2 | | | 15.5 | | 100.0 |
| 1986 | 7.5 | 22.1 | 50.3 | | | 20.1 | | 100.0 |

*Source:* U.S. Department of Energy (1988b).

**Table 3-5.** Estimates of Energy Input to New York Electric Utilities
(Trillions of BTU)

| Year | Coal | Natural Gas | Petroleum | Nuclear | Hydro | Other | Total |
|------|------|-------------|-----------|---------|-------|-------|-------|
| | | | | | Electricity | | |
| 1976 | 147.4 | 5.4 | 547.1 | 173.0 | 321.9 | 0.0 | 1194.8 |
| 1981 | 158.4 | 134.7 | 396.7 | 192.4 | 415.7 | 0.0 | 1297.9 |
| 1986 | 160.2 | 138.4 | 335.4 | 238.7 | 463.8 | 0.0 | 1336.5 |
| **Average Annual Growth Rates (%)** | | | | | | | |
| 1976-81 | 1.4 | 90.3 | -6.2 | | 4.2 | | 1.7 |
| 1981-86 | 0.2 | 0.5 | -3.3 | | 2.9 | | 0.6 |
| **Shares (%)** | | | | | | | |
| 1976 | 12.3 | 0.5 | 45.8 | | 41.4 | | 100.0 |
| 1981 | 12.2 | 10.4 | 30.6 | | 46.9 | | 100.0 |
| 1986 | 12.0 | 10.4 | 25.1 | | 52.6 | | 100.0 |

*Source:* U.S. Department of Energy (1988b).

## Québec Electricity Exports to the United States

Table 3-8 presents total electricity exports from Québec to the United States from 1978 to 1988, as well as the partition into interruptible and firm sales. It can be seen that electricity exports grew from 1.4 TWh in 1978 to reach a peak of 16.4 TWh in 1987 and then fell to 11.9 TWh in 1988. Most of the growth, as well as the decline, was associated with interruptible sales, while firm sales have been steady. Two principal factors explain the growth of Québec electricity exports to the U.S. market: (1) the oil crises of the 1970s rendered obsolete part of the oil electricity generating capacity in the U.S. Northeast, and (2) Hydro-Québec found itself in a surplus situation, which was caused by the completion of the huge Phase I James Bay project and by slow domestic demand growth in the early 1980s. By the mid-1980s, however, these conditions had changed as, first, oil prices declined, and then Hydro-Québec's surplus ended. As a result of these changes, the export price of electricity decreased after 1986, and electricity exports declined in 1988. As shown in Table 3-9, the average export price per KWh for interruptible power fell from US2.25¢ in 1985 to US1.82¢ in 1987, and for firm power from US3.05¢ to US2.48¢.

According to Hydro-Québec's recent development plan (Hydro-Québec 1989), interruptible exports are forecasted to end in 1989 (though they will most probably continue at a much lower level to accommodate short-term opportunities). Premier Bourassa's proposal to increase electricity exports concerns firm electricity, and this is reflected in Hydro-Québec's plan to export some 21 TWh by 2000.[8] Given such a plan, what are the prospects for future electricity exchanges between Québec and the United States?

## MARKET INDICATORS AND ELECTRICITY EXPORTS

Québec electricity exports to the United States have grown in the 1980s under favorable conditions created by Québec's electricity surplus situation and by the imbalance of the generating mix in the U.S. Northeast. Due to strong economic growth and the stabilization (or even decline) of real energy prices, demand for electricity has increased significantly in New England and, to a lesser extent, New York over the past decade. This increased

---

8. This represents 3,500 MW capacity with a load factor of 70 percent. See Hydro-Québec (1989).

**Table 3-6.**  Forecasted New York Power Pool Generating Capacity (Summer)[a]
M W

| Year | Nuclear | Coal | Petroleum | Hydro | Other[b] | Total |
|------|---------|------|-----------|-------|----------|-------|
| 1988[c] | 4774 | 4813 | 12779 | 4975 | 4572 | 31913 |
|      | (15.0) | (15.1) | (40.0) | (15.6) | (14.3) | (100.0) |
| 1990 | 5583 | 4813 | 12898 | 4978 | 6344 | 34616 |
|      | (16.1) | (13.9) | (37.3) | (14.4) | (18.3) | (100.0) |
| 1995 | 5583 | 4813 | 12898 | 5036 | 7930 | 36260 |
|      | (15.4) | (13.3) | (35.6) | (13.9) | (21.9) | (100.0) |
| 2000 | 5583 | 4813 | 12898 | 5374 | 7681 | 36349 |
|      | (15.4) | (13.2) | (35.5) | (14.8) | (21.1) | (100.0) |

a. Figures in parentheses are percentages.
b. Other includes wood, natural gas, purchases from independent producers and other electric public utilities, and imports.
c. January 1, 1989, figures.

*Source:* NYPOOL (1988, 47).

**Table 3-7.**  Available Energy by Source in Québec
(Trillions of BTU)

| Year | Coal | Natural Gas[a] | Petroleum[b] | Electricity[c] | Total |
|------|------|----------------|--------------|----------------|-------|
| 1976 | 19.9 | 84.7 | 1108.0 | 319.0 | 1531.6 |
| 1981 | 14.0 | 118.7 | 919.5 | 410.5 | 1462.7 |
| 1986 | 18.1 | 184.2 | 625.1 | 520.2 | 1347.5 |
| **Average Annual Growth Rates (%)** | | | | | |
| 1976-81 | -6.7 | 7.0 | -3.7 | 5.2 | -0.9 |
| 1981-86 | 5.2 | 9.2 | -7.4 | 4.9 | -1.6 |
| **Shares (%)** | | | | | |
| 1976 | 1.3 | 5.5 | 72.3 | 20.8 | 100.0 |
| 1981 | 1.0 | 8.1 | 62.9 | 28.1 | 100.0 |
| 1986 | 1.3 | 13.7 | 46.4 | 38.6 | 100.0 |

a. Includes gas plant NGLs.
b. Refers to refined petroleum products, coke, and coke-oven gas.
c. Includes hydro and nuclear.

*Source:* Adapted from Statistics Canada, no. 57-003, Table 1 (1976) and Table 7b (1981, 1986).

demand has put more and more pressure on available generating capacity. Planned additions to conventional generating capacity (coal, oil, nuclear, hydro, and natural gas) by electric public utilities in the U.S. Northeast are almost nil (NEPOOL 1988; New York Power Pool 1988). How will the growing demand be satisfied? Projected sources of supply include conservation, demand-side management, non-utility generation and imports.

What is likely to be the contribution of electricity imports from Québec over the next twenty to thirty years? For an economist, an invitation to assess market potential is an invitation to refer to such basic concepts as prices and costs. Economic analysis teaches us that, without impediments, resources tend to flow from low-price areas to high-price ones. This equilibrating mechanism is set in motion by price differentials, and it comes to an end as the price decreases in the importing area and increases in the exporting area under the influence of rising costs of additional supply.

Table 3-10 presents residential and industrial electricity prices in various cities of the region as they existed on May 1, 1988. Clearly, there are fairly large margins in favor of Québec, particularly with respect to Boston and New York. As economic signals, these prices indicate that the province of Québec would be a likely candidate to export electricity to its Canadian and American neighbors to the net economic benefit of all parties involved: lower prices for importing areas and higher value for the exporting one.

As long-term indicators of likely development, the electricity prices displayed in Table 3-10 must be interpreted with some caution. This is particularly so when contracts and projects lasting several decades underlie market operations. Moreover, electricity markets in the U.S. Northeast and the province of Québec have been characterized by imbalances over the past decade. Present electricity prices still reflect these imbalances. Hence, to assess what lies ahead we must also have costs in mind, because costs tell us at what prices new supply can be brought into operation. Unfortunately, it is not easy to find sound cost estimates of new power supplies and particularly of new hydro sites, because each site is unique in terms of design. The main advantage of the cost estimates shown in Table 3-11 is that the U.S. Department of Energy (1987) used a common methodology in the calculations (a single discount rate). According to this study, Québec has about 15,000 MW of capacity at a number of undeveloped hydro power sites, which could supply electricity to Boston and New York at costs significantly lower than coal, the cheapest American alternative. Hydro-Québec (1989, 85) estimated that some 18,000 MW capable of producing 95 TWh remain

**Table 3-8.** Québec Electricity Exports to the United States
MWh

| Year | Interruptible | Firm | Total |
|------|--------------|------|-------|
| 1978 | 722 387 | 679 686 | 1 402 073 |
| 1979 | 4 513 544 | 3 146 352 | 7 659 896 |
| 1980 | 4 908 713 | 3 193 984 | 8 102 697 |
| 1981 | 5 246 298 | 3 071 884 | 8 318 182 |
| 1982 | 5 467 192 | 3 068 597 | 8 535 789 |
| 1983 | 7 162 120 | 3 063 574 | 10 225 694 |
| 1984 | 8 158 622 | 3 081 475 | 11 240 097 |
| 1985 | 6 155 309 | 3 423 202 | 9 578 511 |
| 1986 | 8 514 967 | 4 124 888 | 12 639 855 |
| 1987 | 10 807 000 | 5 610 000 | 16 417 000 |
| 1988 | 6 943 456 | 4 920 769 | 11 864 225 |

*Sources:* 1978-86, Statistics Canada (1987); 1987, Hydro-Québec (1988); 1988, NEB (1989).

remain undeveloped on large rivers in the north and could be brought into production at costs competitive with all other conventional sources (coal, oil, and nuclear). So, given present electricity prices and development costs of new power plants, it appears that Québec will continue to be a significant exporter to the U.S. market in the coming years.

## CANADIAN ELECTRICITY EXPORT REGULATIONS

The electricity export regulatory framework, which was left unmodified in the three decades following the creation of the National Energy Board (NEB) in 1959, is at present undergoing substantial changes. Specifically, Canada and the United States negotiated the Free Trade Agreement, which took effect on January 1, 1989. Chapter Nine of the FTA deals explicitly with energy and, hence, electricity (Government of Canada 1987). Also, the federal government has adopted a market-oriented deregulation policy toward energy since 1985 and the changes resulting from this new approach are currently being implemented for electricity export

**Table 3-9.** Hydro-Québec Electricity Exports to the United States

|                     | GWh    | 000 (US$) | ¢/KWh (US$) |
|---------------------|--------|-----------|-------------|
| **1985 Interruptible** |        |           |             |
| New York            | 5 971  | 133 009   | 2.23        |
| Vermont             | 137    | 4 259     | 3.11        |
| Sub-Total           | 6 108  | 137 268   | 2.25        |
| **1985 Firm**       |        |           |             |
| New York            | 3 000  | 90 825    | 3.03        |
| Vermont             | 476    | 15 129    | 3.18        |
| Sub-Total           | 3 476  | 105 954   | 3.05        |
| TOTAL               | 9 584  | 243 222   | 2.54        |
| **1987 Interruptible** |     |           |             |
| New York            | 5 630  | 88 956    | 1.58        |
| NEPOOL              | 4 770  | 101 535   | 2.13        |
| Vermont             | 407    | 6 629     | 1.63        |
| Sub-Total           | 10 807 | 197 121   | 1.82        |
| **1987 Firm[a]**    |        |           |             |
| New York            | 4 102  | 91 146    | 2.22        |
| Vermont             | 1 505  | 46 621    | 3.10        |
| Sub-Total           | 5 610  | 138 977   | 2.48        |
| TOTAL               | 16 417 | 336 098   | 2.05        |

a.   The sub-total includes a small contract with NEPOOL that does not appear explicitly in the table.

*Source:* Hydro-Québec (1988); 1985 exchange rate: 0.732 (US$) = 1.00 (Can$); 1987 exchange rate: 0.754 (US$) = 1.00 (Can$).

**Table 3-10.**  Electricity Price Comparisons, May 1, 1988
¢/KWh (US$)[a]

| | Residential[b] | Industrial[c] |
|---|---|---|
| Province of Québec | 3.84 | 2.83 |
| Toronto | 5.03 | 3.60 |
| Moncton | 5.41 | 3.57 |
| Boston | 9.06 | 5.48 |
| New York | 12.37 | 6.13 |

a. 1988 exchange rate: 0.839 (US$) = 1.00 (Can$).
b. 1000 KWh, before sales tax.
c. 3.06 GWh, 25 kV, load factor 85 percent, before sales tax.

*Source:* Government of Québec (1988).

**Table 3-11.**  Estimated Electricity Cost Comparisons at Point of Sale in 1985
¢/KWh (US$)

| | Boston | New York |
|---|---|---|
| Hydro Site in Québec | | |
| La Grande 1 | 2.09 | 3.01 |
| Brisay | 2.23 | 3.14 |
| Laforge 1 | 2.25 | 3.15 |
| Grande Baleine | 2.45 | 3.37 |
| La Romaine | 2.47 | 3.40 |
| NBR | 2.48 | 3.37 |
| U.S. Coal | 5.40 | 4.83 |

*Source:* U.S. Department of Energy (1987, Appendices F and G).

regulations. This section briefly summarizes the changes resulting from these two policies and indicates what are likely to be their most significant effects on electricity trade.

### The Canadian Regulatory Framework for Electricity Trade up to December 1988

In Canada, the NEB Act of May 1959 gives the federal government regulatory powers over electricity exports and international transmission lines. Exporting utilities must obtain from the NEB a construction certificate for international transmission lines and an export license for each contract to sell electricity abroad. Provincial governments in general also approve foreign electricity sales undertaken by their government-owned utilities. Imports of electricity to Canada are not subject to regulation.

The NEB determines if electricity for export is surplus, taking into account foreseeable domestic needs and if the selling price is fair and reasonable and in the public interest.[9] To determine if electricity is surplus, the board examines the exporting utility's generating capacity and its commitments. Moreover, the board uses an offer mechanism to verify if a Canadian neighboring utility would be willing to buy in whole or in part the electricity to be sold in the proposed export contract.[10]

The price criteria in the 1959 Act are imprecisely general, and the NEB has developed three guidelines, now part of its regulations, to interpret them:[11]

1. The export price must cover most of the generating costs incurred in Canada.
2. The price must not be less than the price paid by Canadians in surrounding regions for an equivalent service.
3. The price must not be appreciably lower than the cost of the cheapest generating source of the importing utility.

---

9. See Article 83 of the NEB Act. With the Electricity and Liquids Export Act of 1907, the federal government first began regulating electricity exports and international transmission lines. In Article 7 of this Act, the federal government indicated even at that time its concerns that electricity exports be surplus to Canadian needs and that its selling price not be inferior to Canadian prices.

10. The offer mechanism is not formally part of NEB regulations.

11. See NEB regulations, part VI, article 6(2) (Z) (i-ii-iii). The effects of the price guideline on interprovincial and international trade are analyzed in Bernard (1989).

## Effects of the FTA on Electricity Trade Regulation[12]

The main features of the FTA's chapter dealing with energy and electricity are the following:

1.  The prohibition of quantitative restrictions and minimum export and import price requirements, except as permitted by antidumping or countervailing measures (902.2);
2.  the absence of taxes, duties, or charges on exports, except when they also apply to domestic consumption (903);
3.  the proportional sharing of supply with the importing party in a time of GATT-justified trade restrictions (shortages, non-renewable resource management, and price stabilization programs). Such restrictions cannot be accompanied by an export tax, duty, or license (904);
4.  direct discussions between the two parties if one party feels that a federal, state, or provincial regulatory board is taking a decision that runs contrary to the FTA (905);
5.  no restriction on subsidies for oil and natural gas exploration and development (906);
6.  restrictions on exports or imports of energy for narrowly defined national security reasons (907); and
7.  primacy of obligations in the *International Energy Program* agreement over the FTA (908).

In addition to these features dealing with energy trade, the agreement contains features directly related to electricity:

1.  The withdrawal of the NEB's third price guideline;
2.  the acceptance by the Bonneville Power Administration to treat B.C. Hydro on the same footing as other electric utilities outside the U.S. Northwest;
3.  the application of the NEB's electricity surplus test in a manner compatible with the sharing principles governing exports of other energy resources; and
4.  the withdrawal of Canadian and American restrictions on trade in enriched uranium.

In practical terms, it can be considered that free trade already existed in electricity sales before the FTA. In the past, no significant deal between two willing parties has been blocked.

12. This part borrows from Bernard (1988).

Because cross-border electricity exchanges have been characterized by free trade in practice, the agreement as such does not eliminate any significant material constraints. For the present time at least, the withdrawal of the third price guideline, the new sharing rules to be used in the application of the surplus test, and the acceptance by Bonneville Power Authority to give B.C. Hydro national treatment are changes in name only. Furthermore, nothing in the FTA forbids a utility, on the basis of commercial considerations, from charging one price in the domestic market and another price in the export market. However, the FTA does forbid price differences caused by taxes, by export or import price floors or ceilings, and by government quantity restrictions. Given these factors, it is unlikely that the implementation of the FTA alone will be the impetus for expansion of electricity trade.

In the long term, the most significant effect of the FTA on U.S.-Canada electricity trade will probably come from the formal agreement of both countries not to introduce either quantity restrictions or systematic price differentials through export or import taxes or by other means. Although such measures do not exist now, the promise not to introduce them in the future may turn out to be determinant for the signing of long-term sale contracts.

### Streamlined Canadian Electricity Export Regulations

Following the new energy policy orientation of 1985 and 1986, which deregulated oil and natural gas prices within Canada and to some extent for exports, the Canadian Department of Energy, Mines and Resources asked NEB to conduct an inquiry into methods of simplifying electricity export regulations.[13] It should be pointed out that the request made no explicit reference to a more market-oriented approach. The purpose was to simplify electricity export regulations, not to deregulate. After its inquiry, the NEB published a report (1987) that contained a menu of options without indicating any particular preference. After additional consultations, the government presented its new policy for electricity export regulations, which is currently being implemented (Energy, Mines and Resources 1988).

The major points covered by the new policy are as follows:

---

13. Letter of Hon. Marcel Masse, Minister of Energy, Mines and Resources, to the NEB, September 2, 1986.

1. Concerns for surplus power and for just and reasonable prices will remain the cornerstones of the new electricity export regulations.
2. Applications to export electricity will take one of two routes:[14]
    a. if the NEB considers the proposed contract to be in the public interest, a permit for export will be issued without public hearings and without need for federal cabinet approval; or
    b. if the NEB considers that the proposed contract is not in the public interest, it will recommend to the federal cabinet that a public hearing be held. The federal cabinet may reject this recommendation, however, and order a permit to be issued. Otherwise, based on the public hearing, the NEB will either recommend a license to export, which the federal cabinet may or may not issue, or will refuse the application without possibility of appeal to the cabinet.
3. The decision by the NEB to adopt either route will be based in part on provincial practices and procedures concerning cost evaluation and environmental protection.
4. The decisions of the federal cabinet will take into consideration:
    a. unacceptable impacts outside the province of export;
    b. the relevant federal environmental standards; and
    c. the fair market access of neighboring provinces to the electricity proposed for export if needed for their own domestic needs.
5. Negotiated prices will not be made public before approval to export is granted.
6. The maximum duration of an export permit or license is extended to thirty years.
7. The third price guideline is eliminated as negotiated in the FTA.

At this stage, the NEB policy changes appear to be more in the nature of regulation streamlining, as compared to deregulation of electricity exports. Nevertheless, four points in particular are significant: (1) more weight is given to provincial assessments with respect to cost and the environment; (2) there is a greater concern for environmental issues than previously; (3) the policy changes carry the potential for a more active role by the federal cabinet; and

---

14. Only electricity exports are discussed here; the regulations applied to international transmission lines are similar in nature.

(4) there is an emphasis on fair market access to neighboring Canadian utilities for their own domestic requirements without price disclosures before the final decision on export.

## POLICY ISSUES

Electricity exports from the province of Québec to its southern American neighbors have grown in recent years in response to such basic economic incentives as price and cost differentials between the two regions. Considering the same economic indicators today, there appears to be room for a fairly large trade of firm electricity from North to South in the coming years. Will this potential be realized? To some degree, the response depends on various policy issues currently being discussed on both sides of the border. Some of them emphasize the opportunity costs of increasing electricity exports from Québec to the United States. The resolution of these policy issues could result in ceilings being placed on future export levels.

For instance, questions have been raised in the United States, mostly through the efforts of the Coal Coalition, about the fiscal and financial advantages that Canadian public utilities enjoy because they are government-owned. Because of these advantages, Canadian electricity exports are thought to represent unfair competition.[15] The arguments advanced to support this viewpoint are based on the absence of corporate income taxes, preferential rates on debt guaranteed by the provincial governments, and free access rights to hydro power sites. Concerns about fair trading in electricity appear to have little economic foundation when consideration is given to the size of electricity imports in relation to the relevant American markets, the way Canadian electricity exports are priced, and the role played by Canada's National Energy Board.

The first section showed that electricity demand has been growing steadily in the U.S. Northeast over the past decade and that pressure is mounting on available generating capacity (Henderson et al. 1988). Furthermore, local public electric utilities are expected to increase conventional-power generating capacity only slightly by the turn of the century. Due mostly to environmental considerations, it is difficult to build large power-generating facilities in the area. Hence, electricity demand growth is expected to be satisfied by such actions on the demand side as conservation and demand

---

15. This is developed further in Bernard (1988); see also Lee et al. (1988).

management, and on the supply side by plant-life extension, non-utility electricity generation, and imports. The second section described the role Québec could play in imports. However, construction of large sites in Canada gives rise to much the same environmental oppositions as large facilities in the United States. Environmental issues played a major role in the recent rejection by the Maine Public Utilities Commission of the Central Maine Power Co./Hydro-Québec contract. Protectionist measures adopted for these reasons are not forbidden by the FTA.

On the Québec side, there is a significant number of hydro sites that could be developed at costs that are competitive with other U.S. conventional sources of electric power. Three distinct policy directions could be taken in the exploitation of these sites. First, Québec could leave them undeveloped until its own electricity demand warrants development. Such a policy could be justified as a safeguard against future energy crises. Second, the sites could be used to foster industrial development by attracting industries consuming large amounts of electricity (aluminum, for example). And finally, they could be developed for sale in the export market.

These different policy options are considered in a recent report by the Government of Québec's Department of Energy and Resources (1988), which points out that they present different benefits and costs to various groups within the province of Québec. The Government of Québec will most probably follow the policy favored by the majority, and electricity exports are simply one of the possibilities. Of course, parties to the debate must remember the simple rule that electricity dedicated to internal use is not available for export.[16]

## CONCLUSION

Electricity exports from the province of Québec to the U.S. Northeast have grown from a negligible amount in the mid-1970s to become a half- billion dollar business today. This expanding trade came in response to such basic economic incentives as price and cost differentials. Examined today, these same indicators point in the direction of further exports in the form of firm (that is, non-interruptible) electricity. The ongoing regulatory reforms in Canada as a result of both the FTA and the energy deregulation policy pursued by the federal government are creating a framework that should encourage such exports in the long term. In the short

---

16. This point is developed further in Bernard (1986).

term, these regulatory reforms do not appear to make any substantive changes in what was already unfettered trade.

It may turn out that beneficial electricity trade as indicated by price and cost differentials will not materialize because of other competing demands. Concerns about the environment in the United States and Canada, and the husbanding of electricity to foster industrialization in the province of Québec are examples of such competing demands, and they may put a ceiling on future electricity exports.

## REFERENCES

Bernard, Jean-Thomas. 1986. "Avantages et coûts des échanges d'électricité: le cas du Québec." *Revue de l'énergie*, no. 386 (October), pp. 808-14.

——. 1988. "L'accord de libre-échange et l'électricité." *Trade-Offs on Free Trade*. Eds. M. Gold and D. Leyton-Brown. Toronto: Carswell, pp. 249-54.

——. 1988. "U.S. Electricity Imports from Québec and the Fair Trade Issue." *Canadian Public Administration/Administration Publique du Canada*, vol. 31, no. 1 (Spring), pp.43-52.

——. 1989. "Réglementation des prix de l'électricité à l'exportation par l'ONE." Forthcoming in *Actualité économique*.

Bourassa, Robert. 1985. *L'énergie du Nord, la force du Québec*. Montréal: Québec/Amérique.

"Energy, Mines and Resources Canada." 1988. *Canadian Electricity Policy* (September).

Government of Canada. 1987. *Canada-U.S. Free Trade Agreement*. Ottawa: Department of External Affairs.

Government of Québec, Department of Energy and Resources. 1988. *L'énergie force motrice du développement économique: politique énergétique pour les années 1990*. Québec: Direction des communications, ministère de l'Energie et des Ressources.

——. 1989. *L'énergie au Québec, en primeur*, no. 36 (March).

Henderson, Y. K., et al. 1988. "Planning for New England's Electricity Requirements." *New England Economic Review*, (January/February), Federal Reserve Bank of Boston, pp. 3-30.

Hydro-Québec. 1988. *Historique financier et statistiques diverses 1983-1987*. Montréal.

——. 1989. *Plan de développement d'Hydro-Québec 1989-1991. Horizon 1998*. Montréal (March).

Lee, H., N. Forter, and T. Parson. 1988. "Canadian Electricity Imports: An Assessment of the National Security, Economic and Environmental Implication." Working Paper #B 88-06, Energy and Environmental Policy Center, John F. Kennedy School of Government, Harvard University (April).

National Energy Board. 1989. *Exports and Imports of Electric Energy*. Ottawa.

National Energy Board. 1987. *The Regulation of Electricity Exports*. Report of an inquiry by a panel of the National Energy Board following a hearing in November and December 1986, Ottawa.

National Energy Board Act. 1959.

NEPOOL (New England Power Pool). 1989. "NEPOOL Forecast Report of Capacity, Energy, Loads, and Transmission, 1989-2004" (April 1).

NYPOOL (New York Power Pool). 1988. *Electric Power Outlook 1988-2004*. A Report to the Planning Committee of the New York Power Pool (April).

Statistics Canada. *Quarterly Report on Energy Supply-Demand in Canada*, no. 57-003.

Statistics Canada. *Electric Power Statistics*, vol. II, no. 57-202.

U.S. Department of Energy. 1987. *Northern Lights: The Economic and Practical Potential of Imported Power from Canada*, DOE/PE0079. Washington: DOE Office of Policy, Planning and Analysis (December).

———. 1988a. *Annual Outlook for U.S. Electric Power 1988, Projections Through 2000*, DOE/EIA-0474 (88). Washington: DOE Energy Information Administration (August 24).

———. 1988b. *State Energy Data Report Consumption Estimates 1960-1986*, DOE/EIA-0214(86). Washington: DOE Energy Information Administration (April 29).

# II DISPUTE RESOLUTION UNDER THE FTA

Even if the FTA involved only an elimination of tariffs on goods, frictions would inevitably develop because trade liberalization causes reallocation of resources, a disruptive process even for the "winners". Add to this the difficulties of defining and measuring trade in services, issues surrounding intellectual property rights, direct foreign investment, differing national approaches to federal versus state/provincial jurisdiction, as well as a host of other complications, and the scope for disagreement widens dramatically. Much of the FTA negotiations were spent on systematizing and making transparent the processes for dealing with disputes arising from numerous possible sources. The papers in this section explain these mechanisms and offer insights as to their serviceability.

In Chapter 4, Frank Stone helps put the FTA's dispute resolution provisions into perspective by reviewing the long and volatile history of efforts by the United States and Canada to liberalize trade. Stone reminds us that, prior to the implementation of the FTA, the General Agreement on Tariffs and Trade (GATT) served as the principal vehicle for the liberalization of trade between the two countries. Thus, it is not surprising that the basic principles of dispute resolution embodied in the FTA are largely based on those incorporated in the GATT. Of course, the dispute resolution mechanisms in the FTA considerably broaden and extend those in the GATT, and tailor the process to better fit the bilateral relationship. Despite the elaborate institutional setup, Stone cautions that the process is far from comprehensive, and that it should be viewed as a well-intentioned starting point from which more appropriate processes can evolve.

This note of caution is repeated with added force in Chapter 5 by William S. Merkin. After reviewing the general dispute resolution procedures in Chapter Eighteen of the FTA, Merkin outlines several extant sources of friction between Canada and the United States. Three points emerge from this analysis. First, as Stone points out, the dispute resolution mechanisms of the FTA are not comprehensive. Second, we must remember that the FTA was negotiated and enacted amid several pending trade disputes, which may be only partially amenable to resolution under the pact. And third, despite the best efforts of the agreement negotiators, differences of interpretation of the lengthy agreement have already surfaced, and will continue to be a source of friction. Given these considerable challenges, Merkin expresses the hope that both sides realize that an imperfectly operating agreement is clearly preferable to a collapse of the pact.

Jack R. Miller deals with possible private-sector initiatives to settle disputes in Chapter 6. He reasons that such alternative dispute resolution (ADR) procedures can reduce the current and likely strains on the official FTA mechanisms. In addition, he argues that active pursuit of ADRs is a logical extension of the spirit of the FTA, and may serve to reduce tensions by avoiding brinkmanship, thereby increasing the chances for constructive solutions. As compelling as his arguments are on their own, they receive an added measure of urgency in view of the warning lights that the Stone and Merkin chapters flash for us.

# 4 INSTITUTIONAL ELEMENTS AND DISPUTE RESOLUTION UNDER THE FTA

*Frank Stone*

The Canada-U.S. Free Trade Agreement (FTA), which was approved by Congress and the Canadian Parliament in the autumn of 1988, and which came into force at the beginning of January 1989, introduces a wholly new legal and institutional structure for the management of trade and economic relations between the two countries. The FTA is comprehensive and complex. It creates a classic free trade area as envisaged and permitted by Article XXIV of the General Agreement on Tariffs and Trade (GATT); and it creates as part of the overall package of commitments a new structure of bilateral institutions, including new and novel procedures to assist the resolution of bilateral disputes. These institutional structures and the dispute resolution procedures are examined below. First, however, it is useful to review briefly previous institutional structures, or the lack of them, in the bilateral trade and economic relationship, and to take note of the nature and purpose of the FTA.[1]

## BACKGROUND

It is remarkable that historically there have been so few legal and institutional arrangements in economic and trade areas of a

---

1. Subsequent references to the FTA are taken from Government of Canada, *Canada-U.S. Free Trade Agreement*, Ottawa: Department of External Affairs (1987).

bilateral nature between Canada and the United States in view of the massive scale, the complexity and the closeness of their relationships in these areas, and the importance of two-way trade and investment for each country. The Reciprocity Treaty in the mid-nineteenth century, which removed tariffs on cross-border trade in so-called "natural products," but not generally manufactured goods, was short-lived and contained no provisions for joint institutions of any kind. After its abrogation by the United States in 1866, prompted in part by a resurgence of protectionist pressures after the Civil War, no formal trade arrangement between the two countries existed for a period of about eighty years. The reversal of U.S. trade policies in the early 1930s, and the adoption of the 1934 Reciprocal Trade Agreements Act under the Roosevelt administration, led to the bilateral Canada-U.S. trade agreements in 1935 and 1938. These established nothing in the way of joint institutions. Following World War II, the 1938 agreement was in effect suspended when the GATT came into force.

Since 1948, the GATT has served until the present as the main Canada-U.S. trade agreement, as well as the main trade agreement of the two countries with all other GATT member countries. The GATT system contains quite well developed institutional elements for the resolution of disputes, for continuing consultations among member countries, and for the analysis of international trade and trade policy, as well as performing its central functions as an evolving body of trade rules and a framework for trade liberalization. A very large part of Canada-U.S. trade relations has been managed, relatively successfully, within the GATT. Other multilateral institutions such as the OECD, the IMF, and the World Bank have similarly served and will continue to serve as frameworks for Canada and the United States to deal with a variety of economic issues of bilateral interest, as well as broader international interest. By contrast and until now, the strictly bilateral agreements and institutional arrangements in trade and economic areas have not only been few in number, but have provided almost no mechanisms of any formal kind for the ongoing management of Canada-U.S. relations in these areas.

During the 1950s and 1960s, a "Joint Ministerial Committee on Trade and Economic Affairs" met regularly to consider problems in the bilateral relationship and to try to resolve disputes as they arose. This body played an essentially consultative role, and while it served a useful purpose for many years, it lacked any special legal framework within which it could address particular issues or disputes. Over time, it became increasingly difficult to assemble so many busy ministers and secretaries in one place at one time; and the media tended to play up its failure to deal effectively with current problems and disputes, thereby exacerbating them. Meetings of this body were discontinued after 1970.

The need for more effective bilateral institutions to manage the economic and trade relationship was widely discussed before and during the negotiations for the Free Trade Agreement. Quite specific proposals for creating a joint economic or trade commission were made in 1979 by the Honorable Donald MacDonald and in 1983 by Senator George Mitchell of Maine. In 1979, the joint committee of the Canadian and the American Bar Associations recommended the creation of formal arbitration mechanisms for the settlement of trade and other disputes. The author of the present paper put forward proposals for the creation of a joint economic and trade commission, modeled to some extent on the International Joint Commission that was created by the Boundary Waters Treaty of 1909. None of these proposals, however, stirred much enthusiasm in the Ottawa or Washington bureaucracies.

Thus, the bilateral trade and economic relationship continued until the present to be managed through traditional diplomatic channels, or within the framework of the GATT. It is important to bear in mind, in this regard, that the Free Trade Agreement will not replace the GATT, but rather it complements and extends the GATT obligations between the two countries; indeed, many articles of the FTA incorporate by reference GATT rules and obligations. Also, as members of a free trade area, as distinct from a customs union, Canada and the United States are free to pursue their separate, individual trade policies toward third countries and to maintain their separate tariffs on imports from third countries. They will also retain their separate membership and pursue their own interests in the GATT.

In recent years, both Canada and the United States have made good use of the GATT facilities to help resolve bilateral disputes and will doubtless continue to do so. But the GATT procedures will not be available to deal with issues that are particular to the FTA, because they are generally limited to disputes over measures that are covered by GATT rules. The FTA creates a new set of institutional arrangements and a new set of procedures to deal with issues arising from its operation. These new institutions and procedures need to be viewed in the broader context of the nature and purpose of the FTA, and as part of the larger package of rights and commitments.

## MAIN FEATURES OF THE FTA

To begin with, the FTA requires the elimination at once or in stages of all tariffs on goods sold across the border that meet its rules of origin; and it calls for the elimination of most nontariff barriers to cross-border trade, with the notable exception of trade in some important sectors of agriculture that are covered by domestic support programs.    The elimination of these barriers will complete a process of cross-border trade liberalization that has been underway since the mid-1930s under the bilateral agreements of 1935 and 1938 and under the GATT since 1947.

Secondly, the FTA reaffirms and in many areas extends the GATT rules governing cross-border trade, as these have been set out in the GATT Articles and have evolved over time.    New rules are included in the FTA, for example, governing trade in certain service sectors and foreign investment; these go beyond any of the GATT rules, although attempts are now being made in the Uruguay Round to create GATT rules covering these sectors, and the FTA may point the way to rule-making in GATT.    As discussed below, the FTA made no changes to the countervailing and antidumping systems of the two countries, but it calls on the two governments to develop over five or possibly seven years new rules to deal with dumping and countervailing duties as they will apply to cross-border trade.

Thirdly, the FTA sets in place new institutional arrangements to help manage the future trade relationship, and a new set of rules and procedures for the resolution of disputes.    These elements of the FTA need to be examined in the context of the nature and purpose of the FTA as a whole, which is to create and maintain a free trade area between the two countries.    The institutional provisions are not free-standing, but are enshrined in an FTA that has been approved by Congress and by Canada's Parliament; and they are part of a broader set of commitments to build the Canada-U.S. free trade area.

It may be noted here that the articles of the FTA that create new institutional structures and establish new dispute resolution procedures simply provide a base, and in many respects a fragmentary base, upon which these institutions and procedures can operate in the future.    The process of institution building will necessarily be evolutionary.    In this regard, it is noteworthy that the elaborate institutional structures of the GATT, and its well developed dispute resolution processes, have evolved over time on the far more slender base of GATT Articles XXII and XXIII.

## DISPUTE RESOLUTION PROVISIONS

The institutional provisions of the FTA cover a complex and interrelated set of new arrangements, which include:

1. The new Canada-United States Trade Commission;
2. the Secretariat;
3. Chapter Eighteen dispute resolution procedures;
4. Chapter Nineteen dispute resolution procedures;
5. nullification and impairment dispute provisions (Article 2011); and
6. joint arrangements for unfinished business.

### The Canada-United States Trade Commission

This body, created by Article 1802, consists of two cabinet-level representatives or their designates: the Canadian Minister for International Trade and the United States Trade Representative. It has a very broad mandate to supervise the implementation of the FTA, to oversee its future implementation, to resolve disputes over its interpretation and application, to review its functioning at least once a year, and to consider any other matter that may affect its operation. The Commission also plays a central role in the operation of the procedures for the resolution of disputes, other than disputes over the use of countervailing and antidumping duties. The Commission may establish ad hoc or standing committees or working groups, and may seek advice from non-governmental sources. With a few specified exceptions, its decisions will be by consensus.

It is clear that this body is directly responsible to, and will take direction from, the two governments; it is in no way an independent body or "third party," such as the International Joint Commission that was created by the 1909 Boundary Waters Treaty or the GATT Secretariat. Those third-party elements, however, are not absent in the FTA; as will be discussed below, they come into play when independent dispute panels are established under Chapters Eighteen or Nineteen. But it will be the two governments, as distinct from the Commission, that will play the predominant role in the operation of the FTA. For example, notice of measures that may materially affect its operation are given by one government to the other directly, not to the Commission; and initial consultations on such measures are carried out directly between the two governments, with the Commission becoming involved only if these direct government consultations fail to resolve an issue.

Of potential significance is the Commission's authority to establish and delegate responsibility to ad hoc or standing committees or working groups, and to seek the advice of nongovernmental individuals or groups. This provision could play a useful role in the avoidance of disputes by providing alternative opportunities for the input of outside advice on bilateral trade issues, in addition to inputs obtained by the governments from their own domestic constituents. This provision might also provide opportunities for involving provincial and state governments in the operation of the FTA. It is possible, although perhaps not likely, that the two federal governments will see the need in the future for some kind of standing advisory boards with mixed federal, provincial and state, and private-sector representation, analogous to the advisory boards that have been used quite successfully to assist the International Joint Commission in its work under the 1909 Boundary Waters Treaty.

### The Secretariat

The FTA does not give the Commission any staff or resources of its own, underlying its role as an arm of the two governments. However, Article 1909 will establish a permanent Secretariat to service the panels and committees established under Chapter Nineteen to deal with antidumping and countervailing duty issues; and this Article states "the Secretariat may provide support for the Commission . . . if so directed by the Commission." It seems unlikely that the Secretariat will, in the near future, play any kind of independent role in the broader operation of the FTA. No such role is suggested by the text of the FTA as it stands, which places the Secretariat firmly under the control of the two governments, with separate offices in Ottawa and Washington. However, it is possible that over time the two governments may find a need for equipping this body with a larger mandate to assist in the operation of the FTA, for example, in monitoring and analyzing economic and policy developments affecting bilateral trade, assisting ongoing consultations between Ottawa and Washington, and serving as an advisory body to the independent dispute panels.

Secretaries of the Canadian and American section of the binational Secretariat were appointed within a month or so after the coming into force of the FTA. The announcement of the appointment in Ottawa simply noted that the Secretariat would provide administrative support to dispute settlement panels, established under both Chapters Eighteen and Nineteen, and that all requests for review and other consultations under Chapters Eighteen and Nineteen should be filed with the Secretariat.

### Chapter Eighteen: General Dispute Procedures

There are essentially two basic systems for the resolution of disputes under the FTA: the general one, which is provided for under Chapter Eighteen, and the particular one in Chapter Nineteen to deal with disputes over final decisions on antidumping and countervailing duties, as well as to review any proposed amendments to either country's countervailing duty or antidumping duty laws. In addition, the FTA leaves open the option for the submission of bilateral disputes to the GATT for resolution, and this option could be followed where disputes arise over measures covered by GATT Articles, although the GATT and FTA processes cannot be pursued over the same issue at the same time. The GATT member countries would be unlikely to accept a submission over a dispute arising solely out of the operation of the FTA where no GATT obligation was involved, unless the measure under dispute affected the interests of other GATT members.

Under Chapter Eighteen, each country must provide written notice to the other of "any proposed or actual measures" that might materially affect the operation of the FTA (1803.1). Either country may request consultations on such measures proposed or taken by the other, whether or not it has been notified (1804.1). These provisions for advance notification and consultation, if they are respected, represent an important advance in the bilateral trade relationship, and they are also an advance beyond any such obligation under the GATT rules. They embody a principle in the bilateral relationship that was recommended nearly a quarter-century ago by Ambassador Heeney and Ambassador Merchant to Prime Minister Pearson and President Johnson in 1965, but which was never taken seriously.

If a dispute arises over a proposed or actual measure taken by either country, it may be settled by direct consultations between the two governments (1804), but either party may refer it to the Commission for resolution (1805), and the Commission may call upon technical advice or the assistance of a mediator acceptable to both sides (1805.2). These efforts by the Commission essentially represent additional but joint efforts by the two governments to resolve a dispute through direct consultation between themselves. If such further efforts fail, the provisions in Chapter Eighteen for calling on the assistance of a five-member independent panel can be invoked to resolve the dispute.

The five panel members are drawn normally, but not necessarily, from a roster that has now been prepared and agreed to by the Commission, that is, by the two governments. The panelists are to be chosen, in the words of the FTA, "strictly on the basis of objectivity, reliability and sound judgment and, where appropriate, have expertise in the matter under consideration." Panelists may not be affiliated with or take instruction from either government. In this regard, the FTA departs from GATT practice, where panel members are selected by the Director General, in agreement with the parties to a dispute, generally but not always from members of permanent delegations to the GATT in Geneva. The distinction may not be very important, because GATT panel members are selected from countries that have no apparent interest in the dispute, and they serve in their personal capacities, not as representatives of their governments.

The five-member panels include two from each country selected by the governments, with the fifth, who serves as chair, selected and agreed by the two Commission members or, if they cannot agree, by the four panelists. If the panelists cannot agree, the fifth is selected by lot from the roster. This selection process under the FTA should avoid the kind of delay sometime experienced in the GATT when the parties to a dispute cannot agree on the composition of a panel. Moreover, Chapter Eighteen lays down a rigid timetable for the selection process, which cannot extend beyond thirty days.

Unless the two governments otherwise agree, a panel must submit to them within three months an initial report containing "findings of fact, its determination as to whether the measure at issue is or would be inconsistent with the obligations of this Agreement or cause nullification or impairment in the sense of Article 2011" (see below regarding nullification or impairment) as well as "its recommendations, if any, for the resolution of the dispute." The two governments then have an opportunity to comment on these preliminary findings and to raise objections to it. This pause in the process affords a further opportunity for the governments to resolve the issue through direct consultations. The final report of the panel, which presumably would take account of any objections by the governments, must be submitted within a further thirty days. This final report must be made public, along with any dissenting views by panel members, as well as any views on it by the governments if they wish. It should be noted here that when a dispute has not been resolved by direct consultations between the two governments, *either government* can require it to be submitted to the panel process for resolution. This represents one of the most important elements of the FTA dispute resolution process, and is an advance over the GATT process, which at present cannot proceed without the agreement of both parties.

As noted above, the panel's findings and recommendations are advisory, and the two governments are not committed to accept and implement them. However, Chapter Eighteen enjoins the Commission to agree on the resolution of the dispute in ways "which normally shall conform with the recommendation of the panel"; and, "whenever possible the resolution shall be non-implementation or removal" of the measure at issue. If the Commission cannot agree, the injured country is "free to suspend the application of the other Party of benefits of equivalent effect until such time as the Parties have reached agreement on a resolution of the dispute" (1807.9). This ultimate recourse to retaliation is similar to GATT practice, in the case of a member country that fails to implement a dispute panel's recommendations that have been approved by the GATT Council. With few exceptions, GATT panel recommendations have been accepted and implemented by the member countries concerned, although both Canada and the United States have failed to implement certain recommendations of GATT panels in recent years that involve bilateral disputes.

Chapter Eighteen provides for "binding arbitration" in two circumstances, making use of the panel process. One is when both governments have agreed to submit a dispute "for binding arbitration on such terms as the Commission may accept" (1806.1). In this event, a panel is established in the manner discussed above. It may be assumed that both governments, in submitting a dispute for binding arbitration, are prepared to accept and implement the arbitration panel's recommendations. The penalty for non-implementation, however, is similar to the penalty for non-implementation of recommendations by other Chapter Eighteen panels: if the two countries "are unable to agree on appropriate compensation or remedial action, then the other Party shall have the right to suspend the application of equivalent benefits of the Agreement to the non-complying Party" (1806.3).

The binding arbitration process also applies to disputes over "emergency" import measures taken pursuant to Chapter Eleven after these are actually imposed (1806.1). These are measures designed to provide temporary protection to a domestic industry that is being seriously injured by an unexpected increase in competition from imports; they may take the form of additional customs duties or quantitative restrictions. Under GATT rules, these measures are supposed to be imposed on a nondiscriminatory basis against all imports of the product concerned; and both Canada and the United States have on occasion imposed such restrictions in the past against imports from each other, as well as imports from other countries. Chapter Eleven represents a limitation of the rights of the two countries to impose "emergency" or "safeguard" restrictions on cross-border imports of the kind permitted under GATT Article XIX.

Under Chapter Eleven, special rules will apply to the use of such emergency measures on cross-border trade during the transition period to 1998. If domestic producers are experiencing serious injury from imports from the other side resulting from duty reductions under the FTA, these reductions may be suspended for a limited period of time (three years, but not beyond 1998), or the currently applied most-favored nation rate can be reimposed, subject to compensation to the other country—for example, by speeding up duty reductions on another product. After 1998, no such measures may be imposed on cross-border trade, except by mutual agreement.

In addition, the two countries have agreed to exempt each other from "global" emergency measures imposed under GATT Article XIX, except where the other county's producers are "contributing importantly" to the injury. This is an important provision especially from the Canadian perspective; Canadian exporters of steel, for example, have been threatened with the "side-swipe" imposition of restrictions on their exports to the United States because of injury to American steel producers arising from imports from other countries.

In the future, as noted above, disputes over the use of emergency or safeguard import measures on cross-border trade under the FTA must automatically be submitted for binding arbitration under the panel process. These Chapter Eighteen provisions for binding arbitration go beyond any GATT practices, and they represent a significant development in international trade law that may provide a model for extending this binding arbitration process in other areas of the bilateral economic and trade relationship, as well as on a multilateral basis in the GATT.

As is the case with the GATT process, the dispute panel processes set out in Chapter Eighteen can only be initiated by the federal governments. Also, as in GATT, a dispute panel normally will only receive the views of the two governments. Article 1807.4 states that "unless otherwise agreed by the Parties, a panel shall base its decision on the arguments and submissions of the Parties." There is thus little or no scope in the process for input by the private sector or by provincial and state governments. Moreover, panels are not expected to carry out any independent research or analysis of their own concerning issues under dispute. In this respect, the process appears to be more limited than the GATT process, which allows the panelists to draw on the advice and analytical resources of the GATT Secretariat. This absence of independent research and analytical support could weaken the panel process under Chapter Eighteen. Perhaps in the future the Secretariat might evolve in ways that will allow it to provide such support.

It should be noted that the Chapter Eighteen dispute resolution processes do not apply to disputes over decisions by the Canadian government under the Investment Canada Act on whether or not to permit acquisitions by U.S. citizens of certain business enterprises in Canada, as provided for in Chapter Sixteen (Investment). However, other disputes over investment issues can be submitted for settlement under the Chapter Eighteen processes; the two countries are enjoined to select panelists who are experienced and competent in the field of international investment, and panels dealing with investment disputes are to "take into consideration how such disputes before it are normally dealt with by internationally recognized rules for commercial arbitration" (1608.4).

Similarly, disputes over financial services covered by Chapter Seventeen may not be submitted for settlement under the Chapter Eighteen processes (1801.1). Chapter Seventeen calls on the two parties to make public and allow opportunity for comment on legislation and proposed regulations regarding any matter covered by the chapter. Either party may request consultations at any time regarding a matter covered by Chapter Seventeen; and the consultations will be carried out between the Canadian Department of Finance and the United States Department of the Treasury (1704).

### Chapter Nineteen: Disputes over Countervailing and Antidumping Duties

As noted above, the FTA makes no changes in the countervailing or antidumping systems of the two countries as these affect bilateral trade, although the FTA calls for such changes in the future. One of its most widely discussed provisions requires the establishment of a joint working group to develop a new system of bilateral rules to govern the use of subsidies and the use of antidumping and countervailing duties; and the two countries have undertaken to develop "a substitute system of rules" within a five-year period that may be extended to seven years (1906 and 1907).

Chapter Nineteen creates a process for the use of independent joint panels to perform two quite distinct functions with respect to the use of antidumping and countervailing duties. One will be to review and issue "declaratory opinions" on any amendments to the current antidumping or countervailing laws of either party. The other will be to review and make binding decisions with respect to final orders under the antidumping and countervailing duty systems of either country.

The procedures for the creation of binational panels under Chapter Nineteen are distinct from but quite similar to the procedures for the creation of panels under Chapter Eighteen. The two countries in consultation with each other have developed a roster of fifty persons "of good character, high standing and repute" who also have a general familiarity with international trade law; they may not be affiliated with either government nor take instructions from them. When panels are established, each government appoints two members, normally from the roster; the two governments must agree on the fifth member, and if they cannot agree, the fifth member is selected by the other four or, failing agreement by them, is selected by lot. A majority on every panel must be lawyers, and the panelists must choose one of them as chairperson.

In the event either side amends its current antidumping or countervailing duty laws, the other may require the establishment of a binational panel to review and pass judgment on the amendment. The panel must be established within two months, and it will review the changes and issue a declaratory opinion as to whether these changes meet certain specified conditions. The changes can only apply to imports from the other country if the country is specifically named; the other government of the amendment must be notified in advance; and on request, the two governments must consult on the amendment in advance. Moreover, any amendments must be consistent with GATT rules, the GATT Antidumping Code, and the GATT Subsidies Code; and the amendments must also be consistent with "the object and purpose" of the Free Trade Agreement, which in this context is to liberalize cross-border trade while maintaining effective disciplines on "unfair" trade practices (1902).

The proceedings of the panel are confidential, unless the two governments decide otherwise. Its decisions are to be based solely on the arguments and submissions of the two governments, a condition that would seem to place some constraints on the ability of these panels to influence the development of trade law in these areas. The panel must issue an initial opinion within three months from the date of its establishment, and either government may make objections at this stage but cannot halt the process. The panel must issue its final declaratory opinion within the next month and a half. Unless the two governments otherwise agree, the declaratory opinion is made public, along with any dissenting opinions of its members and any views either governments may wish to express. If the panel recommends modification of the amendment at issue, the two governments must consult on ways of achieving a mutually satisfactory solution. If they cannot agree, and if no modification of the amendment is made within nine months, the other country is free to make comparable changes to its own law or, indeed, it may terminate the FTA itself.

Panels established under Chapter Nineteen can also be called on to carry out the quite different function of reviewing final decisions by administrative agencies in either country on the use of antidumping and countervailing duty measures. The Canadian and American systems are quite similar, but not entirely the same. They both provide for the imposition of these special import duties when an imported product is found to be dumped by the exporter or subsidized by governments, and when such imports are determined to cause "material injury" to domestic producers of a similar product. Decisions as to whether an imported product is dumped or subsidized are made in Canada by the Department of National Revenue and in the United States by the Department of Commerce; decisions as to whether domestic producers are injured by such imports are made in Canada by the quasi-independent Canadian International Trade Tribunal and in the United States by the quasi-independent International Trade Commission. Final decisions of these bodies could in the past be appealed for judicial review in Canada to the Federal Court of Appeal and in the United States to the Court of International Trade, with a further right of appeal to the Court of Appeals for the Federal Circuit.

Under the FTA, these appeal processes are replaced by reviews by the binational, independent Chapter Nineteen panels. These panel reviews will be limited to determining whether the final decisions of the administrative agencies were in accordance with the currently applicable antidumping or countervailing duty law of the importing country concerned. A request for a panel review must be made within thirty days after the final decision in question. The request must be made by one of the governments, either on its own initiative or upon the request of a person who would otherwise be entitled to appeal the decision to a domestic court (1904.5). The binational panel is required to apply the laws and standards of judicial review of such cases that are applicable in the country concerned (1904.2 and 1904.3). These laws and standards are somewhat different in Canada and the United States. The reviews by the panels are not confined to hearing and receiving information from government witnesses; persons who would otherwise have standing to appear in a judicial review by a domestic court also have the right to attend and be heard.

The panel must issue its decision within 300 to 315 days of the request for a panel. It may uphold the final decision, or it may remand the decision to the relevant agencies with specific instructions (1904.8). The panel decisions are binding on the agencies (1904.9). In extraordinary circumstances, if either government considers the panel review has been biased or is in other ways faulty, it may request that its decision be reviewed by an "extraordinary challenge committee" consisting of three members drawn from a ten-member roster of former or current Canadian superior court judges or U.S. federal court judges. This committee must render its decision within thirty days; its decision is binding for both governments and cannot be further appealed.

To implement these provisions for binational panel reviews, both countries had to make a number of changes in their domestic laws. In addition, these Chapter Nineteen provisions for binational, independent review of antidumping and countervailing duty cases represent for both countries a significant advance in their approaches to international discipline over their domestic trade policies. Decisions of government departments and agencies in sensitive trade policy areas can and probably will be reversed as a result of binding determination of independent binational panels playing a "third party" role.

As noted above, reviews by these panels are limited to final decisions of administrative agencies, and not to decisions at earlier stages, and as well they are limited to considering the conformity of such decisions with domestic laws. Nevertheless, the existence of the new Chapter Nineteen panel review procedures is likely to influence the decision-making process of the domestic administrative agencies from the beginning, and may also constrain the initiation of requests by domestic industries for antidumping and countervailing duties. While these Chapter Nineteen procedures are applicable only for the interim five- to seven-year period, pending the adoption of a substitute set of rules to govern antidumping and countervailing duties, they will provide a model and precedent for a future and more permanent set of Canada-U.S. rules to govern these systems as they apply to bilateral trade.

### Article 2011: Nullification and Impairment

Article 2011 contains provisions for dealing with disputes over actions by one or other of the countries that may be consistent with the terms of the FTA, or be outside the scope of the FTA, but which nevertheless may "nullify or impair" the benefits that could have reasonably been expected to be gained from the FTA. In these circumstances, Canada or the United States could invoke the provisions of Article 1804 for joint consultations to resolve the issue and, if these do not succeed, the panel process for dispute resolution as provided in Chapter Eighteen can be invoked. With the agreement of the two countries, the issue can also be submitted to the binding arbitration process under Chapter Eighteen. These provisions relating to nullification and impairment of benefits do not apply to disputes over antidumping and countervailing duty cases, or amendments to legislation in these areas, which are covered by Chapter Nineteen. The nullification and impairment provisions in Article 2011 are in line with principles long accepted in trade agreements; they are embodied in GATT Article XXIII, upon which the GATT dispute panel procedures have largely been built.

### Joint Arrangements for Unfinished Business

The FTA has put in place joint arrangements for continuing consultations and other work on a variety of matters covered by it, in addition to the working group established under Chapter Nineteen, which is to advise on a substitute system of bilateral rules to govern subsidies, unfair pricing policies and the use of countervailing and antidumping duties. These other joint arrangements include the following:

1. A working group to review levels of government support for wheat, oats, and barley, and compulsory binding arbitration to determine these levels (Annex 705.4);
2. a joint committee to monitor and report on progress in the further elaboration of technical regulations and standards with respect to agricultural products (Article 708 and Annex 708.1);
3. a total of eight working groups on technical regulations and standards in the field of agriculture (Article 708);
4. a consultative mechanism to review the implementation of provisions relating to the temporary entry of business persons from one country into the other (Article 1503);
5. a select panel on North American automotive trade and production (Article 1004);
6. a joint advisory committee on outstanding issues related to television retransmission rights (Article 2006.4);
7. consultations on uniform administration of customs measures, and notification and consultation prior to major changes in such measures (Article 406 and Annex 406);
8. consultations on regulatory matters in the field of energy (Article 905);
9. a review of compliance with agreed professional standards and criteria for architectural services by a special committee established for this purpose (Annex 1404); and
10. a review of Canadian plywood standards by a special group of experts if this issue is not otherwise resolved (exchange of letters attached to the FTA).

## CONCLUSION

Clearly, the FTA's detailed institutional elements for dispute resolution have been carefully designed and go well beyond past provisions, including those incorporated in the GATT. As disputes develop and are brought under the aegis of the FTA, the strength and utility of these mechanisms will be tested. In the process, the merits of the current measures will become apparent, but deficiencies are also likely to emerge. To the extent the institutional elements allow for the flexibility to deal with unforeseen difficulties, the best intentions of the architects of the Free Trade Agreement can be realized. Beyond this, it is worthwhile remembering that, however carefully constructed the institutional and dispute resolution provisions of the FTA are, their success will call for close cooperation between Canada and the

United States in managing their future trade and economic relationships within the new free trade area context. As well, these mechanisms will almost certainly evolve over time, as they are put into practice, and will play a major role in the new bilateral relationship.

# 5 THE RESOLUTION OF DISPUTES UNDER THE CANADA-U.S. FREE TRADE AGREEMENT

*William S. Merkin*

Among the most significant accomplishments in the U.S.-Canada Free Trade Agreement (FTA) are the dispute settlement provisions found in Chapter Eighteen.[1] This chapter establishes a framework for the resolution of all trade disputes arising between the United States and Canada under the FTA, other than matters covered under Chapter Seventeen (Financial Services) and Chapter Nineteen (Binational Dispute Settlement in Antidumping and Counter-vailing Duty Cases). In fact, during the brief period since the FTA was implemented, even non-FTA-related disputes are being discussed in relation to the provisions of Chapter Eighteen.

The procedures established in Chapter Eighteen are drawn from those in the GATT, with modifications intended to facilitate and expedite the settlement of trade disputes between the two countries. Bilateral Canada-U.S. trade relations in the period prior to the initiation of the free trade talks were characterized by a never-ending series of disputes and irritants. It is hoped that the procedures established in Chapter Eighteen will provide for the expeditious and effective resolution of disputes arising under the FTA.

Given both its wide scope and pivotal role in dealing with Canada-U.S. trade disputes, Chapter Eighteen of the FTA is the focus

---

1. References to the FTA are taken from *U.S. Canada Free Trade Agreement,* Washington, DC: U.S. Government Printing Office (1988).

of this paper. A summary of the principal provisions of Chapter Eighteen is presented first, followed by a survey of several current disputes that have come under, or could conceivably be addressed by, the Chapter Eighteen mechanisms. On the one hand, immediately after the implementation of the FTA, the Canadian government requested consultations, as provided for under Article 1804, on two trade issues. By contrast, though the United States did not immediately file any formal complaints under Chapter Eighteen, three trade-related concerns loom as possible dispute resolution candidates under Chapter Eighteen, and thus warrant examination.

## SUMMARY OF CHAPTER EIGHTEEN PROVISIONS

Article 1801 provides for the application of the conflict resolution provisions of Chapter Eighteen to disputes arising between the United States and Canada with respect to the interpretation or application of any portion of the FTA, except Chapters Seventeen and Nineteen. These provisions would also apply to complaints by either government regarding actions the other has taken, or is proposing to take, that would nullify or impair benefits that the complaining party could reasonably expect to accrue to it under the FTA.

If one government believes that the other has taken an action inconsistent with both the FTA and the GATT, it must select either the FTA or the GATT as the exclusive forum in which to pursue its complaint. Based on that selection, the complaining party will proceed to dispute settlement under the procedural rules applicable in the relevant forum (Chapter Eighteen for a proceeding under the FTA).

Article 1802 establishes a binational "Commission" (the Canada-U.S. Trade Commission), headed by the cabinet officer in each country principally responsible for international trade. In the United States, this is the U.S. Trade Representative, and in Canada, the Minister for International Trade. The Commission will oversee the implementation and further elaboration of the FTA and resolve disputes arising under the FTA. The Commission is empowered to fashion its own rules and procedures, and may make a decision only where both sides agree with respect to the particular matter.

Article 1803 requires one government to notify the other in writing of any measure that it adopts that may "materially affect the operation of the Agreement." However, such notice is not to be construed to indicate that the measure in question is inconsistent with the FTA. Pursuant to Article 1804, the two governments may consult with respect to any issue arising under the FTA; whether or not the matter has been the subject of consultations under Article 1803. Proprietary or confidential information exchanged during the course of such consultations is to be treated on the same basis as it was treated by the government providing the information.

If the two governments cannot resolve a particular matter within thirty days after consultations have begun, either side may refer the issue to the Commission for resolution under the terms of Article 1805. Unless the two sides agree otherwise, the Commission must convene in ten days to consider the matter. The Commission may draw upon experts or mediators to assist in resolving the controversy. If the dispute cannot be resolved by the Commission within thirty days, it may be referred to binding arbitration under the provisions of Article 1806. However, in the case of unresolved disputes regarding actions taken under Chapter Eleven (Emergency Action), which governs safeguard measures, the Commission is required to make such a referral. Once an arbitral panel has found that an action is in conflict with the FTA, and absent an agreement between the governments on an appropriate settlement, the finding must be implemented, or retaliation in the form of suspension by the injured party of equivalent FTA benefits is authorized.

Article 1807 sets out procedures governing the establishment and operation of panels of experts that, upon request of either government, are to hear those controversies that the Commission does not refer to binding arbitration. Panels are to be composed in each particular case of five independent experts drawn, whenever possible, from rosters maintained by each government. Two of the panelists will be selected by each side. A fifth panelist is to be chosen by lot from the governments' roster whenever neither the Commission nor the four panelists are able to make such a choice. Unless the Commission agrees otherwise, each panel will be free to establish its own rules of procedure and must base its decision on the arguments and decisions of the government. In every case, each side is guaranteed at least one appearance before the panel and the right to make written submissions and to offer rebuttal arguments.

Within three months after the selection of its chair, the panel is to present its preliminary report. That report will contain findings of fact and a determination concerning whether the measure at issue is inconsistent with a provision of the FTA or would cause a "nullification or impairment" of the benefits that a party could reasonably have anticipated under the FTA. In addition, the panel is to include in its preliminary report any recommendations that it may have to resolve the dispute. Where feasible, the two governments are to be provided an opportunity to comment on the preliminary report before it is made final. If the Commission so requested at the time the panel was established, the report will also contain the panel's views with respect to the adverse trade effect on the complaining party of any measure deemed to be inconsistent with the FTA.

Each side is afforded fourteen days in which to present written objections to the Commission and the panel with respect to any portion of the panel's preliminary report with which it disagrees. Upon receipt of such objections, the panel may seek the further views of the governments and revise its report, which shall be issued in final form within thirty days following the issuance of the preliminary version. Absent an objection by the Commission, the final report will be made public.

When the Commission receives the final report, it is required to resolve the dispute, normally in conformity with the panel's recommendation. Whenever possible, the Commission is to resolve the dispute by agreeing that the measure in controversy will be removed or, where the dispute involves a proposed measure, will not be implemented. When that remedy cannot be agreed upon, the Commission shall, where possible, agree upon compensation for the complaining party.

Unless it decides otherwise, the Commission must resolve the controversy within thirty days of receiving the panel's final report. Failing such resolution, the complaining party may suspend the application to the other side of benefits of equivalent effect to those that the complaining party considers were impaired, or may be impaired, as a result of the disputed measure. The suspension of benefits may remain in effect until the two sides resolve the dispute.

Under Article 1808, the two governments will endeavor to formulate a common interpretation of the FTA provisions that come under scrutiny in either country's court or administrative proceedings in those instances in which either government wishes to make its views known to the court or administrative body, or where that body or court solicits a government's views on the subject. Any agreed interpretation is to be submitted by the government in whose territory the proceedings are being conducted, in accordance with the rules of the relevant forum. If the two sides cannot reach agreement on the appropriate interpretation, either government may submit its separate views to the extent and in the manner prescribed for such intervention by the forum.

### CURRENT DISPUTES: Canadian Concerns

On January 2, 1989, the day after the FTA went into effect, the Canadian government requested consultations pursuant to Article 1804 on two issues: (1) the definition of what constitutes wool for the purposes of quotas established under the FTA, and (2) the failure of the United States to implement tariff reductions on softwood plywood, waferboard, oriented strand board, and particle board.

### Wool

The United States and Canada disagree over the definition of wool needed to implement a tariff rate quota on wool apparel made in either the United States or Canada from third-country fabric. The quotas are established in Annex 301.2 under Rules 17 and 18 of Section XI (Textiles and Textile Articles). This dispute exists not because of implementation problems, but because neither side could agree during the course of the negotiations on the appropriate definition of wool to use. Therefore, this case may not be well-suited for reference to a panel because there is no negotiating history by which to judge it.

In calculating the U.S. quota, the U.S. side used available trade data based on the existing definition of wool under the Tariff Schedules of the United States (TSUS). However, on January 1, 1989, the United States converted from the TSUS to Harmonized Tariff System (HTS), which contains a different definition of wool. The Canadian side argues that since both countries now use the HTS, the appropriate definition of wool for purposes of the quota should be the HTS version. Because the HTS version is seen as more liberal than the definition of wool under the TSUS, U.S. textile and apparel interests strongly oppose the Canadian position, making resolution even more difficult.

### Plywood

In an exchange of letters dated January 2, 1988, the Canadian government agreed that Canada Mortgage and Housing Corporation (CMHC) would evaluate C-D grade plywood and decide by March 15, 1988, whether to approve its use in housing financed by CMHC. The exchange of letters further provided that if the CMHC did not grant such approval, the two sides would not begin tariff reductions on plywood and other related products until a review of the CMHC evaluation by an impartial panel of experts acceptable to both sides.

Unfortunately, in the view of U.S. negotiators, the CMHC never undertook the independent evaluation of C-D grade plywood that had been anticipated. Instead, the CMHC merely announced that C-D grade plywood did not meet current Canadian standards, a fact well known in both countries. Canadian authorities, in attempting to justify the actions of the CMHC, now argue that the evaluation promised in the exchange of letters was completed, and therefore an impartial panel of experts should be convened to review CMHC's decision.

Congressional and administration reaction to the Canadian actions have been quite negative. The United States believes that the evaluation called for in the exchange of letters was never undertaken by CMHC; therefore, the U.S. is refusing to proceed with the tariff reduction on plywood and related products. Section 201 (c) of the U.S. implementing legislation significantly limits the President's ability to reduce these tariffs unless and until common performance standards for the use of softwood plywood and other structural panels in construction application in the United States and Canada are adopted and incorporated into U.S. and Canadian building codes.

A binational panel of experts has been appointed to develop these common performance standards; however, the work will likely take several years for completion, if the exercise is successful. In the interim, Canada argues that the United States has no unilateral right to withhold the tariff reductions on plywood and related products. They maintain that a decision can only follow a review of the CMHC evaluation by a panel of experts as provided for in the exchange of letters. The United States counters that Canada did not fulfill its commitment to evaluate C-D grade plywood in the first place, and there is therefore nothing to review. This case is likely to be the first referred to a Chapter Eighteen panel.

## CURRENT DISPUTES: U.S. Concerns

Although the United States has not formally filed any complaints yet under Chapter Eighteen, there are three areas of concern to the United States regarding Canadian compliance with the FTA that have been raised with Canadian authorities: (1) provincial implementation of the alcoholic beverage provisions, (2) uranium upgrading requirements, and (3) retransmission.

### Alcoholic Beverages

Chapter Eight of the FTA provides for significant changes in provincial practices and policies affecting the sale and distribution of wine and distilled spirits. Due to the complexity of the provincial liquor board practices, the extent to which Canadian provinces are fulfilling their obligations to eliminate discriminatory listing, pricing, and distribution practices remains unclear. In fact, there are some reports that some provinces have actually expanded their discrimination during the past year. It will likely take most of 1989 just to sort out the situation.

What was clear during the first three months of operation of the FTA was the defiance by the government of Ontario to the FTA measures affecting wine. Despite the importance of the issue, the United States reacted cautiously to this situation due to continued assurances from the federal government in Ottawa that Ontario would be brought into compliance with the FTA very quickly. In fact, it was not until mid-March that agreement was reached between Ottawa and Ontario to resolve this impasse. In return for Ontario's compliance with the FTA, Ottawa has agreed to contribute substantial funds for the marketing of Canadian wine. While the anticipated April 1 compliance with the FTA by Ontario should remove a potentially serious bilateral dispute, further difficulties in the areas of provincial responsibility are likely to arise again.

### Uranium Upgrading Requirements

Annex 902.5(2) of Chapter Nine of the FTA requires Canada to exempt the United States from its uranium upgrading policy. However, the Canadian interpretation is that the United States is exempt from the requirement that uranium be upgraded in Canada prior to export only in the following cases: (1) when the uranium is converted and enriched in the United States (regardless of the ultimate destination), or (2) when the uranium is converted and ultimately consumed in the United States. The uranium would not be exempt when it is converted in the United States and enriched and consumed elsewhere. This exclusion has some commercial significance to the U.S. conversion industry. Canada argues that paragraph 3 (b) of Article 902 permits Canada to require uranium exported to the United States be consumed in the United States or suitably transformed prior to subsequent export to another country.

The U.S. view is that the specific language of paragraph 2 of Annex 902.5 should take precedence over the more general language of paragraph 3 (b), which was developed originally to deal with the question of oil exports. Paragraph 2 of Annex 902.5 states that the United States is to be exempted from the export restrictions. Maintaining the restriction against U.S. processors that convert uranium oxide to uranium hexaflouride for subsequent re-export is not, from a U.S. perspective, consistent with the language of paragraph 2 of Annex 902.5.


**Retransmissions**

Article 2006 of the FTA provides that a United States or Canadian copyright holder must receive "equitable remuneration" whenever a broadcast containing a program in which he holds a copyright is simultaneously retransmitted in unaltered form in an area outside that in which the broadcast can generally be received. The provision was designed to eliminate the unreimbursed retransmission, principally by Canadian cable companies, of U.S. television broadcast signals.

The United States currently provides a right of equitable remuneration under a compulsory licensing royalty scheme established pursuant to the Copyright Act. The FTA requires Canada to have fully operational by January 1, 1990, an equivalent system for granting remuneration to U.S. copyright holders.

However, Canada's draft regulations prepared last year gerry-mandered the definition of "local" signal (where no remuneration is necessary) to include metropolitan Toronto. This means that the largest single Canadian market, Toronto, would be outside the scope of the requirement to provide compensation. U.S. officials believe strongly that this approach significantly guts the benefits anticipated from implementation of Article 2006, and indeed is contrary to assurances given during the negotiations. The Canadians argue that the definitions for "distant" and "local" signals contained in their draft regulations are consistent with U.S. practice under the Copyright Act.

## ADDITIONAL CHALLENGES

In addition to the specific disputes described above, both U.S. and Canadian officials have been utilizing the forum provided by the Canada-U.S. Trade Commission to discuss issues that are not directly linked to the FTA, but which have significant importance for the bilateral relationship. Among the areas under discussion are: (1) Canadian concerns over changes in tariff classifications under the new U.S. Harmonized Tariff Schedules, (2) U.S. concerns over the expansion of Canada's dairy quotas to cover ice cream and yogurt, and (3) the U.S. GATT case against Canadian export restrictions on unprocessed fish. The use of the Canada-U.S. Trade Commission for these discussions signifies the importance that both governments attach to a successful and smooth launching of the FTA. It is a clear attempt to contain bilateral differences and irritants before they become public confrontations.

Only time will tell whether the new dispute resolution provisions of the FTA live up to their promise. An effective, timely method for resolving disputes is essential to the long-term success of the FTA. Both governments seem to recognize this, and hopefully will strive to ensure that it works. There really is no other option. Failure to peacefully manage disputes could easily lead to a collapse of the entire foundation on which the FTA is built.

# 6 ALTERNATIVE DISPUTE RESOLUTION IN CANADA-U.S. TRADE

*Jack R. Miller*

One of my early cases, as a practitioner specializing in the resolution of conflicts and the settlement of disputes, concerned the relative merits of American and Swiss circuit breakers. For this case, I cross-examined one of the parties for three days on the design of its circuit breaker. I felt I had won my case in the cloakroom, however, when during a break for lunch the chairman of the tribunal asked me as we were putting on our coats if I really felt that the domestic design was obsolete. I said yes, of course. Later, my Swiss clients were exonerated of dumping duties on the ground that customers had preferred their design.

It was not until 1982, however, that I became cognizant of alternative dispute resolution, which was then in its infancy. I attended the Annual Lectures of the Law Society of Upper Canada and heard a paper by Donald Brown and Peter Alley entitled "Management of Corporate Disputes," which referred me to Roger Fisher and William Ury's (1983) Harvard Negotiation project publication, *Getting to Yes*, subtitled "Negotiating Agreement Without Giving In." Since then, I have voraciously consumed any materials I could find on the subject, and I have begun to apply the knowledge systematically in my law practice. This paper offers insights from my research, reflection, and experience on the potential for the application of alternative dispute resolution (ADR) in Canada-U.S. trade. My purpose is to stimulate and open up a wider view, thereby making a small contribution to enable others to make the most of the Canada-U.S. Free Trade Agreement (FTA).

## ALTERNATIVE DISPUTE RESOLUTION

It is customary to begin an introduction to a relatively new subject with a reference to precedent and tradition. The reference is usually to ancient Greeks; it seems there is nothing that they had not conceived. The purpose is to disarm the listener and lull him into a state of mind reminiscent of Bobby McFerrin's hit song "Don't Worry, Be Happy."

So, first the customary reassurance: we know that most people resolve their disputes themselves. We know that a very high percentage of disputes taken to court are resolved prior to formal adjudication. We know that there is abundant precedent and an effective tradition of people, often with the help of third parties, finding alternatives to formal adjudication themselves.

The purpose of alternative dispute resolution is to speed up and enrich those processes so that more and better settlements occur earlier. Indeed, one could say that any good attorney worth his salt who survives the pressures of private practice regularly engages in alternative dispute resolution without being aware of it, much like the person who did not realize that he was engaging in prose when he was writing something down. ADR has moved on to and up the agenda of both the Canadian Bar Association and the American Bar Association so that one could argue that today it is in the mainstream of the legal profession.

The American Bar Association (ABA) has produced an excellent work on the subject entitled "Alternative Dispute Resolution: An ADR Primer" (1987), which in a concise, readable fashion summarizes the principal alternatives and answers questions frequently asked about ADR. The ABA Primer defines ADR as follows:

> ADR refers to a broad range of mechanisms and processes designed to assist parties in resolving differences. These alternative mechanisms are not intended to supplant court adjudication, but rather to supplement it.

The Primer then lists a number of ADR methods that have some counterparts under the FTA dispute resolution mechanisms. One could argue that the FTA and the GATT dispute resolution mechanisms are themselves ADR, and one might refer to them as "public international law ADR," because the public authorities have a large part and the processes are institutionalized.

Nevertheless, the term "ADR" is ambiguous. Even though it is a handy and catchy reference, the phrase often gives rise to much confusion. The phrase "conflict resolution and dispute settlement," is perhaps more precise. This can be thought of as a spectrum of approaches measured by the degree to which parties resolve conflicts and disputes. At one end, the parties do it themselves. At the other end, someone does it for them. In the middle, the parties do it themselves with the support of others. Furthermore, a distinction can be drawn between "conflicts" and "disputes." A conflict is internal to a person or an institution, whereas a dispute involves two or more persons or institutions. The goal of conflict resolution and dispute settlement is not only to settle the dispute, but also to resolve conflict and get to the bottom of things. That was the good news, the comforting and reassuring part. The bad news is that all is not well and there is a need for innovation to meet needs. This is the challenging part, which sounds the retreat for many.

John W. Burton, who is associated with the Center for Conflict Resolution at George Mason University, in *Resolving Deep-Rooted Conflict—A Handbook* (1987) makes a useful distinction between what he calls "normal conflict," which lends itself to intelligent management, and what he refers to as "deep-rooted conflict," which requires a more considered approach that Burton calls "facilitated conflict resolution." Burton presents an informative history of conflict resolution, which includes resolution at the international level and might well have been the history of conflict resolution in Canada-U.S. trade. For example, Burton notes that "blatant power politics was practiced" at the international level. The purpose of international charters was to curb these practices, but essentially such charters were still based on a power philosophy. This approach has ignored basic needs, and for this reason has proved of limited use.

By contrast, the modern approach is based on the following realistic understanding of the human condition (Burton 1987):

> The awareness of needs which cannot be compromised, cannot be made subject to some legal judgment, cannot be bargained, leads logically to the development of a process that enables parties to conflicts to ascertain the hidden data of motivations and intentions and to explore means by which common human-societal needs can be achieved. As these needs of security, identity and human development are universal, and because their fulfillment is not dependent on limited resources, it follows that conflict resolution with win-win outcomes is possible.

This is really what ADR purports to address and what makes it one of the most exciting technologies of all time.    ADR is adisciplinary, that is, it pertains to no particular discipline but rather to an interaction of disciplines, including those derived from lay experience, because ADR is not only a reform movement within the official justice community of lawyers and judges, but also a grassroots intuitive phenomenon.

I have found validation of my own intuition and experimentation in the works of Burton and others.    Recently, I have been working on the grand-daddy of all deep-rooted conflicts, which also involves North America's original free traders, who, incidentally, continue to assert this right: the deep-rooted conflicts between the aboriginal or indigenous peoples, in particular the Iroquois Confederacy and their neighbors, Americans and Canadians.    I am hopeful these new approaches, which correspond to the traditions of the native people, will bring about some win-win solutions for all concerned within a relatively short time-frame.

## THE FTA ENVIRONMENT

The FTA manages to mention competition and cooperation in the same breath.    Therefore, it is not surprising to find that resolution of disputes is also a prime objective.    The FTA objectives aim both to "facilitate conditions of fair competition within the free trade area" and to "lay the foundation for further bilateral and multilateral cooperation to expand and enhance the benefits of this Agreement." This seems to mean that it is all right for governments to cooperate but not for industries; hence the further objective of seeking to "establish effective procedures for the resolution for disputes."

It is possible that as the FTA is implemented the emphasis will be on cooperation and not competition, because cooperation produces more economic gain than competition.    Even antitrust considerations can be covered by involving all interested parties in the process and by the transparency of the process, although antitrust laws really sanction defects from cooperation and not cooperation itself.

The main disputes that are likely to arise in relation to the FTA can be classified as follows:

1.    The unfair pricing practice known as dumping, which is really uncooperative behavior; in other words, seeking to maximize one's own gain without regard for others;

2.  the distortions of governmental interventions in the economy in the form of subsidies and other measures;
3.  integrity of the FTA, such as respecting the rules of origin, the classification systems, and its intent and purpose; and
4.  elaboration of the agreement; various negotiations and other initiatives and processes to reach a consensus of greater specificity than the present.

It is highly probable that the dispute settlement mechanisms of the FTA will require supplementary mechanisms if the FTA is to achieve its potential. Indeed, the official FTA mechanisms should be reserved for those exceptional cases where the parties need more help, even to the point of having a matter decided for them. Otherwise, parties will come too soon to this process for want of an alternative and will ask too much of the official mechanisms.

Many of the disputes under the FTA are likely to fall into the category of deep-rooted conflicts. The FTA dispute resolution mechanisms are flexible enough that they could in time evolve into processes that meet the needs of groups in society, such as industry and consumers. In this regard, pre-hearing administrative conferences could evolve into facilitated conflict resolution. However, when jobs and plants are at stake it is not an exaggeration to feel in the presence of needs that, in the words of Burton, "cannot be compromised, cannot be made subject to some legal judgment, and cannot be bargained" (1987). Thus, in the short term, the challenge falls to the private sector to facilitate the resolution of these deep-rooted conflicts by the groups themselves.

## FACILITATING CONFLICT RESOLUTION

There are a number of steps that can be taken to move toward filling this gap. First, it is important to focus more on the dynamics of conflict resolution and dispute settlement rather than on the form. What is it in the process that leads to successful resolutions and settlements? To answer this question, we have to hunker down to where the action is. For instance, trade is carried on by business and not by government in North America. Moreover, the number of businesses trading on a daily basis is not as large as we might think. It is important to identify particular individuals and institutions and to think in terms of their interaction.

We know that the workhorses of conflict resolution and dispute settlement are: (1) information exchange, and (2) listening and analysis. We know that emotions are often determined by perceptions, and perceptions are frequently a function of information. Distortions in perceptions can be corrected by information; fears can be released by information. We know that resolutions and settlements are always facilitated by exchange of information. Thus, we could focus on ways to facilitate an exchange of accurate and relevant information in a timely and appropriate manner.

We know that listening is a great healer and validates and informs people. Listening empowers people. We want to empower people. We want them to be free of their fears and to consider alternatives. People who are defending themselves or who are attacking are not listening, and they miss much valuable information. We want them to have the calm to be able to recognize win-win solutions. Listening is an art and a science. In this respect, the work of Carl Rogers (1980) and others has great potential for the resolution of disputes. It is important to tap into it and apply it. In the conventional hearing, a party is "heard" by the tribunal. It is important that in the same manner each party "hears" the other. Listening leads to a well-rounded analysis of the entire situation, which inevitably reveals a range of options. Thus, we should set things up to facilitate listening.

Secondly, it is important to promote and facilitate an interaction among parties to a conflict or dispute where the parties themselves are the central characters and others are the supporting cast. It is useful to think about ways to bring parties together. It may even be worthwhile to think about uniting parties that are not in dispute but that have had disputes in the past and are likely to have disputes again. Often, more can be accomplished when the interaction is not conditioned by a crisis.

In this context, several random thoughts come to mind that are relevant though loosely connected. Resolution and settlement work best when the situation is cast as a common search for solutions and is conducted from particular perspectives rather than the classic adversarial stance. The physical arrangements are important to achieve this effect. The interactive method rather than the Rules of Order method of meeting is more conducive to conflict resolution and dispute settlement. Fisher and Ury (1983) stress the importance of being soft on people while being hard on issues. This formula sounds anodyne (and is, indeed, soothing), but it also involves for many a radical departure from convention.

Finally, we know that there is a natural tendency to disorder, and we have to invest energy to bring about order out of disorder. Stephen Hawking speaks of this in *A Brief History of Time* (1988):

> It is a matter of common experience that disorder will tend to increase if things are left to themselves. (One has only to stop making repairs around the house to see that!) One can create order out of disorder (for example, one can paint the house), but that requires expenditure of effort or energy and so decreases the amount of ordered energy available.
>
> A precise statement of this idea is known as the second law of thermodynamics. It states that the entropy of an isolated system always increases, and that when two systems are joined together, the entropy of the combined system is greater than the sum of the entropies of the individual systems.

Thus, it is perhaps necessary to let go a bit of order in the form of established routine, allow a bit of disorder in the form of parties sorting out a format that works for them, and hope that a new form of order will emerge in the guise of interaction among parties in conflict, so that conflict may be resolved and the parties may make the most of the Canada-U.S. Free Trade Agreement. There may be some confusion, and we may feel uncomfortable, but let us empower the parties, anyway.

## REFERENCES


ABA.    1987.    The Standing Committee on Dispute Resolution. *Alternative Dispute Resolution—An ADR Primer.* Washington, DC: American Bar Association.

Axelrod, Robert.    1984.    *The Evolution of Cooperation.* New York: Basic.

Brazil, Wayne D.    1988.    *Effective Approaches to Settlement: A Handbook for Lawyers and Judges.*    Clifton, NJ: Prentice Hall Law and Business.

Burton, John W.    1987.    *Resolving Deep-Rooted Conflict—A Handbook.* Lanham, MD: University Press of America.

CPR Legal Program.    1987.    *ADR and the Courts—A Manual for Judges and Lawyers.*    Saint Paul, MN: Butterworth.

Fisher, Roger, and William Ury.    1981.    *Getting to Yes—Negotiating Agreement Without Giving In.* Boston: Houghton Mifflin Co.

Hawking, Stephen W.    1988.    *A Brief History of Time—From the Big Bang to Black Holes.* New York: Bantam Books.

Kohn, Alfie.    1986.    *No Contest—The Case Against Competition—Why We Lose in our Race to Win.* Boston: Houghton Mifflin Co.

Maine Law Review.    1988.    *Symposium—Alternative Dispute Resolution in Canada-United States Trade Relations,* vol. 40, no. 2.

Percy, M. B., and C. Yoder.    1987.    *The Softwood Lumber Dispute & Canada-U.S. Trade in Natural Resources.*    Ottawa: The Institute for Research on Public Policy.

Rogers, Carl R.    1980.    *A Way of Being.*    Boston: Houghton Mifflin Co.

*U.S.-Canada Free Trade Agreement.*    1988.    Washington, DC: U.S. Government Printing Office.

# III CANADIAN IDENTITY AND THE FTA

Questions about the economic impact of the FTA were raised during the Great Free Trade Debate of 1988, but these were not at the heart of the battle. Rather, what lead to the election showdown between the Conservatives and Liberals, and what sparked such bitter comment, was the concern that more liberalized cross-border trade and investment would result in the dilution of Canadian national identity as distinct from that of the United States. This concern is certainly not new; indeed, as both chapters in this section make clear, the debate over more liberalized trade with the United States has been a central fact of political life in Canada since the country's founding.

In Chapter 7, Peter Brimelow begins by harking back a century ago to the first Canadian election fought over freer trade with the United States. He finds a number of arguments made at that time by Goldwin Smith applicable to the current debate. Building on Smith's reasoning, Brimelow outlines eight points, two of which in particular stand out. First, because Canada comprises several ethnically and/or geographically distinct regions, there is no more a single "Canadian" identity than there is a single Canadian viewpoint on the impact of the FTA. Second, Brimelow raises the possibility that for some regions of Canada greater integration, on many levels, with the United States may in fact be desirable.

Maureen A. Farrow and Robert C. York review the history of the free trade debate in Canada in Chapter 8. They call attention to the fact that the FTA is essentially an *economic* pact. In their view, the debate surrounding the agreement has to too large an extent focused on noneconomic issues. Nevertheless, the anti-FTA forces did criticize the pact on economic grounds as well. Farrow and York present a clear outline of these arguments and then examine them point by point. They not only conclude that the economic benefits outweigh the costs, they also argue forcefully that the benefits flowing from the agreement will in the long run serve to strengthen the Canadian nation and enhance its sovereignty.

# 7 THE FREE TRADE AGREEMENT: IMPLICATIONS FOR CANADIAN IDENTITY?

*Peter Brimelow*

*Truth, even scientific truth, is merely a special case of the fantastic*
—Ortega y Gasset

I must begin this discussion of the social and cultural considerations for Canada of the Free Trade Agreement (FTA) with the literary equivalent of the Surgeon General's warning. My views are "well outside the bounds of virtually all Canadian political discourse," as Daniel Casse wrote when he reviewed my book on Canada in The *National Interest* magazine in 1987. This does not mean, of course, that I am wrong. Canadian political discourse is peculiarly narrow, for reasons I will discuss later, and, in fact, I am merely following in the footsteps of Canada's preeminent Victorian intellectual, Goldwin Smith, who can be regarded as the Canadian de Tocqueville, and who, in 1891, in the aftermath of the first election fought on the issue of bilateral free trade with the United States— which free trade lost—published his classic *Canada and the Canadian Question,* from which I drew my own book's subtitle (Smith 1971; Brimelow 1987). Nevertheless, experience has taught me to commend my epigraph to the reader.

## FREE TRADE AND CANADIAN IDENTITY: A BRIEF HISTORICAL EXCURSION

Free trade with the United States, of course, is and always has been the single most important economic issue facing Canada. "It is her

105

own soul that Canada risks today," Rudyard Kipling cabled in 1911, on the eve of the second Canadian election fought on free trade (which free trade also lost). "Signing Away Canada's Soul: Culture, Identity, and the Free Trade Agreement," was the title of a *Harper's Magazine* essay that the Canadian novelist Robertson Davies published in January 1989, directly after the Third Great Free Trade Election—which free trade, of course, had finally won.

Goldwin Smith would have viewed all this as patently absurd. "The two sections of the English speaking race on the American continent," he pointed out, ". . . are in a state of economic, intellectual and social fusion, daily becoming more complete" (Smith 1971). And he raised the issue that has earned him nearly a hundred years of obloquy from the Canadian "Nationalists" (1971):

> Whether the four blocks of territory constituting the Dominion [he meant the Maritimes; Ontario and Quebec, alias "Central Canada"; the Prairies; and British Columbia] can forever be kept by political agencies united among themselves and separate from their continent, of which geographically, economically, and with the exception of Quebec ethnologically, they are parts, is the Canadian question.

Who was (and is) right? In retrospect, I think it can be seen that Kipling had at least something of a case. But Davies does not. His attempt to make a case depends on a number of sleights of hand all too familiar to any student of the "Canadian Nationalism" that has dominated the country's public debate for the last generation.

Kipling had something of a case because when he wrote Canada seemed to have a viable alternative, both economically and culturally, to North America. At that time, Canada officially regarded itself as an integral component of the British Empire whose flag it flew. It was part of what Sir Charles Dilke called the "Greater Britain" beyond the seas. A Greater British patriotism permeated Canadian popular culture to an extent that is now completely forgotten. For example, the 1910 Ontario Fourth Reader used in the public schools had on its flyleaf a Union Jack and the motto "One Flag, One Fleet, One Throne," and opened with Kipling's "Children's Song":

> O Motherland, we pledge to thee
> Head, heart and hand through years to be!

and closed with his "Recessional" after 400 pages of British patriotic poetry. It was politically acceptable for a Francophone like Sir George-Etienne Cartier to say, "I am an Englishman who speaks

French," and for Sir Wilfrid Laurier to tell a banquet celebrating Queen Victoria's Diamond Jubilee, "I am British to the core." Canadian cultural heroes like the humorist Stephen Leacock and Colonel John Maclean, founder of the magazine that bears his name and is now identified with a particularly reflexive form of "Canadian Nationalism," were actually outspoken advocates of "Imperial Federation"—the idea, seriously discussed at the turn of the century, that Britain and its Dominions should formally unite, elect representatives to an Imperial Parliament in London and build a wall of preferential tariffs against the outside world. Colonel Maclean even claimed apostolic succession for this policy in the form of an interview with Sir John A. MacDonald, whom he quoted as saying it was just the logical extension of Canada's own confederation.

Goldwin Smith, a liberal anti-imperialist, doubted the strength of this imperial loyalty. "If England ever has occasion to call on her children in Canada for a real sacrifice," he wrote, "she may chance to repeat the experience of King Lear." In this respect, Smith was utterly wrong, as two world wars demonstrated. In World War I alone, Canada put 625,000 men into uniform and suffered 61,000 dead, an astonishing performance for a country of a mere 8 million people.

After 1945, however, Britain effectively vanished from the geopolitical stage. Culturally and economically, there was no longer any influence on Canada to rival that of the United States. Canada's Greater British patriotism was rendered obsolete. This had a number of subtle but far-reaching consequences, one of which was the creation of a new official view of Canada—which, however, was even more at variance with Canadian reality than the old.

## THE PRESENT-DAY CANADIAN REALITY

In this beginning phase of the Free Trade Agreement era, I offer a summary of what I believe the Canadian reality to be. Essentially, I have reconsidered and, I believe, strengthened the arguments I made in my book prior to the national election (Brimelow 1987).

*1. Canada is merely a geographical expression.* For historical reasons, Canada has acquired the legal form of a nation-state, but it is not a nation. In particular, the Anglophone and Francophone communities are growing more separate every year, culturally and even spatially.

Canada's "Nationalists" have developed two basic methods to finesse this embarrassing fact. First, they assert in the face of all evidence to the contrary that the oil and water of English Canadian and French Québécois culture have indeed mixed. Second, they just carry on talking about Canada as if Québec did not exist. Robertson Davies in his *Harper's* essay (1989) favored the latter course, which was particularly inappropriate because Québec was significantly more in favor of the FTA than English Canada. Goldwin Smith, in contrast, laid heavy emphasis on the singularity of Québec, quite rightly as it turned out. He was already aware of both evasive maneuvers, as he showed in this discussion of a precursor of "Nationalism," the "Canada First" movement of the 1870s (Smith 1971):

> Enthusiasm was blind to the difficulty presented to the devotees to Canadian nationality by the separate nationality of Quebec, or if it was not blind, succeeded in cajoling itself by poetic talk about the value of French gifts and graces as ingredients for combination, without asking whether fusion was not the thing the French most abhorred.

2. *There are at least two and conceivably seven incipient sub-nations within Canada.* By far the most important division is that between English Canada and Québec. But there are significant distinctions within English Canada: Ontario; the West with or without British Columbia; the Maritimes, with or without Newfoundland; and the native-dominated North. All these divisions constitute fault lines underlying the Canadian policy.

Sheer size poses a more serious political problem for Canada than is generally recognized. Human communities are centrifugal in tendency. It has been the exception rather than the rule for the great overseas possessions of the European imperial powers to retain political unity after independence. Spanish America, only about a million square miles larger than Canada's 3.6 million, has fragmented into fifteen different countries. But even the proverbially lucky Australians suffered a crisis in the 1930s when Western Australia voted to secede. In the United States, regional or "sectional" tension has been a notoriously important and often dominant political theme (Garreau 1982). A similar torsion is continuously if quietly at work in Canadian politics.

In the short run, the electoral success of the FTA probably tended to alleviate sectional tensions in Canada by appeasing the West, which has historically favored free trade but had previously always been outvoted. In the long run, however, free trade may reduce the sections' economic and emotional dependence on Ottawa—which is certainly why the Parti Québécois supported it. And free trade by itself cannot remove sectional discontent. That much was made clear by the recent crushing victory of the Reform Party candidate in the federal by-election at Beaver River, Alberta. This is the first parliamentary seat gained by Reform, a right-center western particularist group that austerely refuses to run candidates in other parts of Canada. It must now be viewed as a serious threat to the Tories' western contingent, already vulnerable since their leader Brian Mulroney is so preoccupied on reorienting the party to Québec.

3. *Within the Canadian framework, Québec is emerging as a genuine nation-state on the European model.* History does not move in straight lines. There is a cyclical rhythm to Francophone nationalism as well as a rising long term secular trend. Foreign opinion has naturally been fixed on the decline of outright separatism since the defeat of the referendum on sovereignty-association in 1981 and of the Parti Québécois itself in 1985. But this overlooks the fact that the previous quarter-century of turmoil has left the Francophones in total institutional control of Québec, which is now regarded by all segments of Francophone opinion as their political expression. In Ottawa jargon, the *deux nations* concept—the idea that Canada should resolve its internal problems by making Québec a French-speaking enclave within an English-speaking state—has triumphed posthumously over *une province comme les autres*, Pierre Trudeau's view that Québec was just another province and that Francophones should look to all of Canada as their political expression.

The Mulroney government's Meech Lake Accord, the latest of Canada's endless efforts to finalize its constitution, signified the effective abandonment of Trudeau's policy with language recognizing Québec as a "distinct society." But simultaneously, Mulroney has continued and even extended federal institutional bilingualism, which is predicated on the Trudeauvian fantasy that Canada is a bilingual, bicultural society from coast to coast. This contradiction periodically racks Canadian politics. The most recent convulsion occurred shortly after the 1988 federal election invoked the so-called "notwithstanding" clause in Canada's Charter of Rights to override the Canadian Supreme Court and retain its separatist predecessor's legislation aimed at making Québec a unilingual French-speaking society. These convulsions will certainly continue.

The impressive support shown for the Free Trade Agreement by all sections of the Québec elite, in systematic contrast to its

Anglophone counterpart, must be viewed as further evidence of Québec's separate existence as a nation. Québec's attitude suggests that the concerns about "culture" raised by Anglophone opponents of the FTA were misplaced. No community in Canada is more conscious of its cultural identity than Québec. None has shown such willingness to use government power in its defense. Yet none was more enthusiastic about free trade. It must also be noted that the Québécois tend to view English Canadian claims to a "culture" distinct from that of the United States with somewhat unkind derision.

   4. *All of Anglophone Canada is essentially part of a greater English-speaking North American national culture.* Canada is a sectional variation within this supernation, differing in nuance just like the American South, the Pacific Northwest (probably culturally the closest to Canada), or the Upper Midwest. But it shares a core of common values. This, incidentally, is an entirely respectable thing for it to be.

   Goldwin Smith, in other words, was right. The two English-speaking societies are in a state of what he called "practical fusion." Canadian attitudes are not necessarily identical to those of Americans, as Seymour Martin Lipset has demonstrated over the past years. (Note, though, that Lipset [1985] has refined his position: in a recent essay on the subject, he points out that he has "paid more attention here than in my earlier writings to variations between the two Canadian linguistic cultures. The evidence indicates the Francophone Canadians vary more from their Anglophone conationals than the latter do from Americans.")   But it is a question of whether the glass is half full or half empty: seen in a global context, what North Americans have in common is more apparent than what divides them. Of course, Canadian Anglophone intellectuals are typically fairly ignorant of international comparisons. And a good few of them just want to break the glass.

   It took me 100,000 words to support this view of English Canada in my book, a performance which I will refrain from reproducing here. Instead, I will confine myself to a couple of symbolic anecdotes.

   One of the triumphs of Canadian "Nationalism" in the 1970s was legislation preventing the deduction as a business expense of the cost of advertising in *Time* magazine, which at that time published a special Canadian edition in Montréal. This was a tacit subsidy to *Maclean's* magazine, which undertook to transform itself into a Canadian weekly news magazine—itself an indication of the extent to which characteristically American forms are automatically imitated in Canada. Much less known was the unexpected consequence. *Time* magazine fired its Canadian staff and began exporting its U.S. edition to Canada, slashing advertising rates to offset the loss of deductibility and raising the subscription price to slough off uneconomic circulation. Weekly sales fell from some 550,000 to about 365,000, where they stabilized more profitably than before. Apparently, that many Canadians were perfectly happy to buy an American news magazine with no Canadian content at all. Thus, the "Nationalist" triumph had merely succeeded in demonstrating how completely American Canadians were.

In 1982, Prime Minister Pierre Trudeau scheduled three televised "fireside chats" on the economy. He appeared at 7:30 p.m. in Montréal, Ottawa, and Toronto, which of course meant a rush-hour 5:30 p.m. in Alberta and an impossible workday afternoon 4:30 p.m. in British Columbia. Trudeau was famously insensitive to the West—one historian of the Liberal Party has even claimed that he had never been west of Toronto when he became Prime Minister—but on this occasion there was an excuse: chatting any later would have put Trudeau in conflict with the World Series on the American border stations. At such moments of truth, Canadian politicians have no doubts about the cultural identity of their flock.

*5. Canada's political system is badly designed and seriously misrepresents Canadian reality.* The most important flaw is lack of effective regional balance, which has allowed elements in Central Canada to dominate the country since Confederation. But specific institutional factors, such as the parliamentary system itself, are responsible for many Canadian political characteristics that are conventionally attributed to Canada's unique ( = unAmerican) political culture.

At a national level, Canada is a unitary state. It is salutary to reflect that if the United States had the same electoral system, Tom Foley would be Prime Minister—and Jim Wright would have been his predecessor. Foley is, and Wright was, leader of the majority party in the House of Representatives, which like the House of Commons is made up of single-member, first-past-the-post districts of roughly equal size. In both countries, this allows the cities of the East to dominate the spaces of the West.

The American founding fathers were keenly aware of the danger of domination by a tyrannical majority section. They tried to counter it by creating the Senate, to which each state regardless of population was entitled to send two members. This gave the regions power at the federal center. By contrast, the Canadian Senate is appointive and has become moribund.

Historically, Central Canada's domination of Canadian politics is the fundamental reason for Ottawa's prolonged love affair with protection. In effect, the region has been able to force the rest of Canada to subsidize its high-cost industries by keeping out cheap foreign goods. In Public Choice economics, this is called "rent-seeking"—the use of political power to extract rents, subsidies, from the economy. The Maritimes and the West have faced competitive world prices for their raw material exports and uncompetitive Canadian prices for their manufactured imports. The result has been devastating.

Some Canadian free trade advocates believed as recently as the early 1980s that their country's political system had become such a tangle of pathologies that the policy could never be adopted. The reasons for its subsequent success are complicated. One factor must be that the population of the West has finally grown to the point where Canadian politics has become a three-actor system. Free trade was the product of a tacit alliance between the West and Québec. In this sense, it could be argued the FTA itself reflects a shift in Canada's "culture" toward the values of the West.

6. *The political system and Canada's deep divisions, particularly linguistic, have facilitated the growth of an unusually large and powerful "New Class."* This New Class, comprised of civil servants, educators and assorted political and media hangers-on, is the real Canadian Establishment, mediating across Canada's divisions and inventing policies that benefit itself and its clients. One example of such a policy is federal bilingualism, a major social engineering effort that diverts power and perquisites toward the 15 percent of Canada's population that is bilingual, most of whom are Central Canadians. Another example is the National Energy Program, which in effect was an attempt by Ottawa to expropriate the windfall energy profits of the West and to distribute them to Central Canadian client constituencies (Doran 1984). This sort of sectional despoliation is much more difficult in the United States because of its effective Senate. In Australia, the elected Senate blocked the Whitlam Government's very similar lunge at the mineral wealth of Western Australia and was ultimately able to force an election, which Whitlam lost.

7. *The Canadian New Class has developed what Marxists (Joll 1978) call a "dominant ideology," rationalizing and justifying its power, and has been quite successful in imposing it as the Canadian conventional wisdom.* This ideology basically amounts to the direct opposite of everything asserted above. Over the years, it has been identified with the Federal Liberal Party, but it has clear antecedents in the contending

schools of Canadian historiography (Taylor 1982). An important variant of this ideology is "Canadian Nationalism." These sixth and seventh points together are crucial to an understanding of the Anglophone intelligentsia's attitude toward the FTA. Whereas in the nineteenth century the manufacturing industries of Central Canada were the most obvious beneficiaries of rent-seeking, rationalizing their interests in terms of Greater British Imperial patriotism ("The Old Man, The Old Flag, The Old Party" in 1891), in the twentieth century the most prominent rent-seekers were Central Canada's cultural and communications industries, which rationalized their interests in terms of "Canadian Nationalism." The extent of the subsidy goes far beyond quasi-government agencies like the Canadian Broadcasting Corporation and the National Film Board. The late-Trudeau-Applebaum-Hebert Commission on "cultural policy" admitted that "the degree of government involvement in supporting writing and publishing is considerably greater in Canada than in other nations that share our cultural heritage." It observed that even established commercial authors were increasingly applying for state aid.

Few people are capable of sustained conscious hypocrisy. It would be unfair to say that Canada's Anglophone intelligentsia opposed free trade entirely because they feared, probably wrongly, that Ottawa would be obliged to make them face a market test they suspected, probably rightly, they would fail. Many of them no doubt believe their own propaganda, while others are convinced socialists who have taken to heart Waffle leader Mel Watkins' slogan that "Radicalism in Canada has to mean Nationalism."

But this "Nationalism" is manifestly ersatz (which is why I insist on putting it in quotation marks). It is slavishly careful to avoid anything that might be politically inconvenient for the ruling party in Ottawa (parties, strictly speaking, since Brian Mulroney in most respects seems to be attempting to co-opt the historic Liberal coalition). Thus, Canadian "Nationalists" have not complained about the imposition of federal bilingualism, although it obviously disadvantages the fourteen out of fifteen Anglophones who are unilingual. (This conspiracy of silence on bilingualism has been frankly admitted by its supporters [Gwyn 1981]). They have accepted "multiculturalism," Ottawa's programs to subsidize immigrant groups' efforts to retain their identities, although this is logically inconsistent with any preservation of Canada's much-vaunted distinctive culture (and Québec nationalism, which is genuine, insists that immigrants assimilate to the Francophone milieu). And finally, because any mention of the past, particularly English

Canada's British and imperial past, is thought to be distressing to Francophones, Canadian "Nationalists" repress it. In a real if subtle sense, it is the Anglophone rather than the Francophones who are the colonized, censored group in Canada. Thus, Robertson Davies begins his essay with the rhetorical question, "Is Canada a country without a mythology?" announces that "talk of the Canadian soul has [just recently] begun," and makes the usual "Nationalist" noises about Canada's supposedly unique—and certainly uncontroversial— landscape, which turns out as always to mean Ontario's landscape (1989). Maybe this was what Kipling was worrying about in "Recessional":

> Lord God of Hosts, be with us yet,
> Lest we forget—lest we forget.

*8. Canadian politics are surprisingly volatile. Many key Canadian institutions, such as federal bilingualism, date only from the 1960s and the pivotal Prime Ministership of Pierre Trudeau. They may prove merely transitional.* Anyone inclined to dispute this should remember that in the 1983 Tory leadership race, Brian Mulroney flatly opposed bilateral free trade.

Unlike Goldwin Smith, I do not predict that all or any of Canada's provinces will one day enter the American union, although I do think that it would be an absolutely legitimate option for them to consider. But, despite the fact that it has been unfashionable to say so for thirty years, the unmistakable reality is that Canada, arguably including Québec, does have a "special relationship" with the United States. The FTA is one formal expression of this relationship. There could be others—for example, a customs union or a common market. These would constitute what Ottawa enthusiasts for a chimera of an alliance with the European Community in the 1970s were able to call, without having their Canadianness impugned, a "contractual link."

## CONCLUSION

My opinion of the FTA's implications for Canadian culture should now be clear: it has no implications. Trends that are already well-established will continue. This is equally true, as a matter of fact, for the FTA's economic implications. U.S.-Canadian economic integration has proceeded apace despite a generation of "Nationalist" politicking. This supports my contention that the

"Nationalist" objective was not really to truncate the relationship but to tax it. By contrast, bilateral free trade in 1891 and 1911 would have meant some degree of cultural and economic reorientation away from Britain. The magnitude of this shift, of course, is still a matter for argument.

I believe the Great 1988 Free Trade Debate was, up to a point, what psychologists call a "delegate issue"—something that everyone tacitly agrees to discuss so as to avoid really painful and controversial questions. In Canada, such questions are: the emergence of Québec as a French-speaking nation-state; the mounting unfairness to Anglophones of Pierre Trudeau's Official Language policy; the entrenched power of Canada's bureaucracy in an age of privatization; the injustice of Canada's unitary national-level institutions to regional communities like the West. All of them must eventually be answered—but not any time soon, if the professional politicians can help it.

The FTA was marginal rather than radical. But in economics what happens on the margin matters. Goldwin Smith said the slogan "Rich by nature, poor by policy" should be inscribed over Canada's door. In the years since then, the gap between the two countries' living standards and per capita GNP has been persistent and pathetic. Free trade is only one of the policies by which Canada can cease impoverishing itself. But it is a start.

I think Canadian culture will also benefit on the margin. Way back in 1961, the great Canadian economist Harry G. Johnson warned:

> Far from contributing to the growth of a stronger, more independent, and identity-conscious nation, Canadian Nationalism as it has developed in recent years has been diverting Canada into a narrow and garbage-cluttered cul-de-sac.

He was rejected (and indeed reviled). I hope it will not compromise my glacially impartial approach in this paper if I report that those of us who argued with the "Nationalists" in Canada often felt as if we were shoveling garbage. Canadian "Nationalists" will not go away. But their characteristic self-interested self-delusion will in the future be more difficult to maintain.

## REFERENCES

Brimelow, Peter. 1986. *The Patriot Game: Canada and the Canadian Question Revisited.* Toronto: Key Porter. Also published in 1987 by Hoover Institution Press, Stanford, CA.

Davies, Robertson. 1989. "Signing away Canada's Soul: Culture, Identity and the Free-Trade Agreement." *Harper's Magazine* (January).

Doran, Charles F. 1984. *Forgotten Partnership U.S.-Canada Relations Today.* Baltimore: Johns Hopkins University Press.

Garreau, Joel. 1982. *The Nine Nations of North America.* New York: Avon Books.

Gwyn, Richard. 1981. *The Northern Magus: Pierre Trudeau and the Canadians.* Markham, Ontario: Paperjacks.

Johnson, Harry Gordon. 1961. *The Canadian Quandary: Economic Problems and Policies.* Toronto: McClelland and Stewart.

Joll, James. 1978. *Antonio Gramsci.* New York: Penguin Books.

Lipset, Seymour Martin. 1985. "The Cultural Dimension." *Canada and the United States: Enduring Friendship, Persistent Stress.* Eds. Charles F. Doran and John H. Sigler. Englewood Cliffs, NJ: Prentice-Hall Inc.

Smith, Goldwin. 1971. *Canada and the Canadian Question.* Toronto: University of Toronto Press.

Taylor, Charles. 1982. *Radical Tories: The Conservative Tradition in Canada.* Toronto: House of Anansi.

# 8 ECONOMIC, SOCIAL, AND CULTURAL POLICY INDEPENDENCE IN THE POST-FREE TRADE ERA: A VIEW FROM CANADA

*Maureen A. Farrow and Robert C. York*

Canada has just passed through an historic period in its political and economic dimensions. The Great Free Trade Debate about comprehensive free trade with the United States set off an emotional outpouring from Nanaimo, B.C., to St. John's, Newfoundland. The no-holds barred dogfight spawned an unprecedented level of national disunity, and an election was fought over it. Indeed, the federal election in November 1988 was the direct result of a move by the Liberal opposition leader, John Turner, who, through the Liberal-dominated Senate, managed to block the initial passage of the free trade legislation. Opponents of the Free Trade Agreement (FTA) argue that it is nothing short of the "Sale of Canada Act," while proponents counter that it is the means through which Canadian employment and incomes will grow. Both sides agree, however, that the FTA is an historic document whose real and symbolic effects will persist for decades, and possibly for centuries.

The removal of virtually all tariffs and many nontariff barriers to Canada-U.S. trade—the means through which access to each other's market is improved, and the *raison d'être* for the FTA—has largely been ignored. Instead, attention has been focused on emotional issues that are in fact peripheral to the FTA, but are at the heart of the "Canadian way of life." These issues are the political, social, and cultural implications of the treaty.

In this paper, we address the opponents' concerns in the Great Free Trade Debate from the perspective that through this agreement (and through a continued commitment to multilateral trade liberalization), Canada can maintain and, more importantly, enhance its position as a sovereign and prosperous nation.

In Section I we set the stage by presenting a brief history of Canadian trade policy. The opponents' arguments in the debate are laid out in Section II. In Sections III through V, we spell out the reasons why we feel there still will be a "Canadian way of life" even after free trade, and explain why the FTA does not have dire consequences for Canada, politically, socially, and culturally. The paper closes with a brief conclusion in Section VI.

## I.   A BRIEF HISTORY OF CANADIAN
## TRADE POLICY: SETTING THE STAGE

The FTA does not have Canada sailing into uncharted waters. With a few twists and turns, Canada-U.S. trade relations have evolved through increasing interdependence.  Since the National Policy of 1879—the high water mark of Canadian protectionism with high tariff walls and import-substitution—Canadian trade policy has been one of increasing trade liberalization along two distinctive paths: through successive bilateral arrangements with the United States and multilaterally through the General Agreement on Tariffs and Trade (GATT).

The first experience in freeing trade between Canada and the United States occurred with the Reciprocity Treaty of 1854, which allowed for free trade in a range of manufactured and primary products.  The Treaty was abrogated by the Americans twelve years later, and it was not until 1911 that the United States approached Canada to renegotiate the lowering of tariff barriers.  Ironically, there was a Canadian election fought on the U.S. proposal in which the free-trade-supporting Liberal government lost to the Conservatives, who campaigned on the platform of "No Truck or Trade with the Yankees."

Two significant bilateral treaties were signed with the United States in the 1930s, and in 1944 duties were removed in both countries on all agricultural machinery and implements trade, and there has been free trade in these products ever since.  In 1965, the Automotive Products Trade Agreement (auto pact) became a center-piece of Canadian commercial policy and a symbol of Canada-U.S. trade relations.

Along the multilateral trade path, Canada has worked toward removing trade barriers to foreign markets since 1947, when it became a founding member of the GATT. There have been seven rounds of GATT negotiations, with the eighth, the Uruguay Round, due to be completed in 1990. The two most successful rounds—the Kennedy Round (1964-1967) and the Tokyo Round (1973-1974)— resulted in across-the-board tariff cuts of about 35 percent. During this time, many Canadian firms rationalized by reducing their product lines and increasing production runs of those that remained. The result was a more competitive Canadian economy and the volume of exports and imports increased dramatically in real terms over this period.

In the latter part of the 1970s and early 1980s, Canadian governments abandoned temporarily the outward-looking trade policy stance that had served Canada well since the National Policy. This was the time of the OPEC energy crisis and the high tide of Canadian nationalism. Three policies set the tone for the period. First, there was a strong sense of vulnerability to energy shocks brought on by the rapid rise in the price of oil. This prompted calls for a "Made in Canada" energy policy—domestic energy prices, self-sufficiency, and a buyout of foreign-owned firms operating in Canada—and the subsequent adoption of the National Energy Program.

Second, the rapidly rising stock of foreign direct investment in Canada, particularly from the United States, led to feelings of anti-Americanism and the creation of the Foreign Investment Review Agency (FIRA). It was FIRA's job to review all applications for foreign direct investment in Canada and often to require investment-related performance requirements as a condition of investment.

Third, Canadian nationalists believed then and now that Canadian culture was threatened by U.S. mass media, especially television. Thus, Bill C-58 was introduced in the Canadian Parliament providing tax deductions to Canadian firms for television advertising directed at Canadian audiences, but denied these deductions to U.S. stations broadcasting in Canada.

While the effect on "Canadianism" and Canadian culture from these policies can be debated for a long time, the economic effects are clear. There was a sacrifice of some of the gains from trade, a deflection of foreign direct investment away from Canada, and a loss in Canadian competitiveness in world export markets. In the recession of 1981-1982, Canada's GNP declined further than any OECD country. This astonishing prospect forced Canada to again look outward and to adopt an internationalist policy stance—the Free Trade Agreement implemented in January 1989 attests to that position.

## II. THE CANADIAN FREE TRADE DEBATE: "CANADA AT STAKE"

The recent free trade debate—which is still going on in Canada, although at a much lower level of intensity—began back in 1985 when the Progressive Conservative government took free trade with the United States seriously. By the time trade negotiations actually began in mid-1986, solid opposition to the initiative had formed a well-organized front involving church and women's groups, cultural and environmental groups, and several major labor unions, and somewhat later in the debate included the Liberal and New Democratic opposition parties. Scarcely a day went by without Canadians being besieged by critics predicting the loss of control over domestic energy, social, and economic programs, the loss of Canadian culture, and ultimately the loss of Canadian sovereignty, and to many what assuredly would mean the political union of the two countries.

The most surprising and no doubt the most disappointing feature of the debate was the way in which the antagonists and protagonists talked past each other rather than to each other. Also disappointing was that much of the discussion was focused on fears about myths and assumptions about the FTA and not about the FTA itself.

The free trade debate took on two discernable phases. In the first phase, prior to the conclusion of the negotiations, opponents developed several basic arguments:[1]

1. Canadian industry cannot compete tariff-free with the United States, so free trade would lead to massive unemployment.
2. The small cut in tariffs would not benefit consumers much.
3. Canadian culture would be taken over by "Americanism."
4. Canadian social policies would have to be reduced to U.S. levels to remain competitive.
5. The FTA would result in an inflow of U.S. direct investment and thus a sell-out to the Americans.

---

1. This list and the next one are drawn from Lipsey (1988) and Lipsey and York (1988).

6. U.S. branch plants located in Canada would relocate back to the United States, leaving Canadians as "hewers of wood and drawers of water."
7. The FTA would mean a fortress North America, with critics charging proponents of the deal as being continentalists, and not the true internationalists they claimed to be.

When the negotiations were completed and the FTA was finally published, the debate focused on several aspects of the deal:

1. The FTA prevents Canadian governments from developing future policies with respect to foreign investment, energy, water, the environment, and regional development subsidies.
2. The inclusion of services in the FTA provides a back-door through which lower-quality U.S. services will lead to the erosion of high-quality Canadian social services.
3. It does not increase Canada's security of access to the U.S. market, because it leaves U.S. trade laws intact.
4. The cultural exemption and retaliation clause makes implementing measures to encourage Canadian culture more difficult.
5. The nullification and impairment clause will allow U.S. firms providing social services to enter Canada, or to obtain compensation if entry is denied.
6. The FTA restricts Canada's rights in the GATT.

## III.  SOVEREIGNTY

### The Agreement in Context

To understand why the FTA does not entail a serious loss of Canadian sovereignty as the critics have claimed, it is important to understand its scope and coverage.   The FTA is a commercial agreement covering trade in all goods and some services, provides rules for investment, and requires the commitment to develop bilateral rules for trade remedies.   It is more comprehensive than the U.S.-Israel Agreement, which is confined mainly to trade in goods, but it is not as encompassing as the European Community, which, being a common market, requires common commercial policies and the free movement of factors of production, as well as the harmonization of many government policies.

### How Does the FTA Preserve Canadian Sovereignty?

All international agreements involve some restriction on domestic policies. That is their purpose. What is important is that what is given up does not impair policy independence in areas deemed important to domestic concerns. There are essentially two ways through which the FTA can affect Canadian sovereignty:[2] (1) through direct constraints on government policies, and (2) through indirect constraints or policy harmonization pressures, which the FTA does not call for, but which it nonetheless causes.

### Direct Constraints

The FTA allows Canada (and the United States) to preserve its policy independence by mandating very few direct constraints and through the fundamental principle on which it is based—national treatment. The principle of national treatment—which is also the guiding principle underlying the GATT—allows each country to implement any policies it wishes and they can be different from those of the other country. All that the FTA requires is that neither country use these policies to discriminate on the basis of nationality. For example, Canada can adopt strict environmental laws while the U.S. does not, as long as these laws are applied equally to both Canadian and U.S. firms operating in Canada. This principle is extended to all levels of government in both countries, except where the provinces and states are explicitly excluded from the FTA's obligation, as in the case of government procurement policies. It is left for each country's federal authorities to ensure that all subnational jurisdictions comply to the terms of the treaty whenever necessary.

The principle of national treatment applies to almost all trade in goods, to many services that are covered by the FTA, and to some types of foreign investment. These provisions apply only to *new* rules, laws, and regulations and *not to existing ones*—the so-called grandfathering provision—even if they offend the principle of national treatment. The FTA also exempts from the national treatment provisions a range of sensitive industries, most importantly from our perspective in this paper, all cultural industries (broadly

---

2. This draws heavily from the arguments laid out in the Appendix to Lipsey and York (1988) and C.D. Howe Institute (1986).

defined) and services such as medical, legal, and child care, and all government-provided health, education, and social services.[3]

In their detailed tour through the FTA, Lipsey and York (1988) find only two provisions that pose any "real" constraints on Canadian sovereignty. First, in the energy chapter, Canada (as well as the U.S.) accepts that the price of energy exports will be determined by market forces, and not through government fiat (through export taxes, for example). But this does not mean that Canada cannot follow its own domestic energy policies, such as controlling the rate of extraction, taxing energy resources at the well-head, or subsidizing Canadian energy users if it so wishes. Both countries also agree to proportional sharing of energy (and all other traded) resources in times of shortage, declared at the exporting country's request. Again we do not agree with the critics that this is a serious restriction on Canadian governments, because Canada (and the U.S.) are already committed to such sharing rules generally under the GATT, and through the International Energy Agreement in the case of oil.

Second, in the investment chapter Canada agrees to end the use of investment-related performance requirements attached to U.S. investment in Canada. This is a direct constraint on Canadian sovereignty, the importance of which is debatable, however, and depends largely on the extent to which one trusts or mistrusts foreign capital. We take the view that rules and regulations are needed to control the behavior of firms, but they need not discriminate between those owned by Americans and Canadians.

Canada also agrees to phase out the review of U.S. direct and indirect takeovers of firms worth in excess of $150 million (Canadian). This again places some constraints on Canadian policymakers who wish to control U.S. investment in Canada in small- and medium-sized businesses. However, from our perspective we see little in the way of Canada's giving up anything of significance, because two-thirds of all nonfinancial capital is still reviewable and, more importantly, this includes the really large takeovers that often become a national concern.

### Harmonization Pressures

Even if the FTA does not explicitly put *de jure* pressure on Canadian sovereignty, it can create them *de facto*. These are the policy

---

3. For a more detailed account of the FTA's exemptions from national treatment, see Lipsey and York (1988) or the Free Trade Agreement (Government of Canada 1987).

harmonization pressures the critics claim Canada will necessarily have to accede to in order to remain competitive with U.S. firms in a liberalized trading environment. These policies range from the lowering of Canadian environmental regulations to the adoption of U.S. social policies. We are not convinced by these harmonization arguments, because they derive little support from the experience of other countries, from Canada's own history, or from economic theory. Consider the following points outlined by Lipsey and York (1988):

1. Seventy-one countries are currently involved in trade liberalizing arrangements and none has complained of lost policy independence. High- and low-spending countries have benefited from free trade, as well as rich countries and poor countries. So the evidence from other countries suggests that free trade does not constrain domestic social policies.

2. Canada has been liberalizing trade with the United States since the 1930s, to the extent that today about 80 percent of bilateral trade is tariff-free. If trade liberalization leads to policy harmonization, then Canadian and U.S. policies should be 80 percent harmonized already. Clearly they are not. Canadian policies can thus remain distinct in the face of liberalizing trade.

3. Harmonization pressures relate to the movement of factors of production, and not the ease with which goods and services can be traded. The FTA affects the latter, but not the former.

4. The desire of Canada to have an extensive social safety net that increases Canadian costs vis-à-vis the United States would bring about a compensating depreciation of the Canadian dollar to retain Canadian competitiveness. As long as the exchange rate is free to adjust to market forces, it will provide the key mechanism that allows diversity in social policies to exist among trading nations.

We add a further point to the list put forth by Lipsey and York. The harmonization debate in Canada is misguided because it ignores the increasing globalization of many markets. The term "globalization" refers generally to a market place for standardized products that is worldwide in nature. It relies on enormous scale economies in production, distribution, marketing, and management. It also has important implications for the volume of world trade and the patterns of trade. This is best exemplified by John Helliwell (1989), who suggests that the "longer term trade balance changes are likely to come not from Japanese imports of standard U.S. goods, but from the establishment of plants outside Japan to make 'Japanese' goods for Japanese and world consumption."

It is presumed in the free trade debate that Canadian policymakers will be forced to adopt U.S. policies and regulations. But because of the increasing globalization of markets, the driving force behind harmonization is the international market place, not the United States. Thus, it makes little sense for Canada to adopt U.S. trade policies in many cases. For example, in financial markets where globalization has raced ahead, the harmonization pressures facing Canada are driven by Tokyo and London, not New York. In this sector, Canada has moved far ahead of U.S. regulation and, in fact, the United States before too long will be forced by global realities to move financial regulations—the Glass-Steagall Act, separating retail and investment banking, and the McFadden Act prohibiting interstate banking—more in line with Canada's.

So what does globalization mean for a small country like Canada? Helliwell sees globalization as an opportunity to be exploited; to be successful, countries must remain flexible enough to adapt to change and to see it as an opportunity and not as a threat (1989, 74):

> If the national policies could embrace and exploit the inevitable globalization of economic activities, this will permit the removal, even if gradually, of a number of the more wasteful and debilitating national or regional policies, designed in the mistaken hope that 'defense' or 'counter-attack' is a feasible strategy for any country, and especially a relatively small and open one like Canada, to respond to changes in the global economy.

## IV.  THE SOCIAL POLICY DEBATE

The social policy debate revolves around three main aspects of the FTA: (1) the harmonization pressures it allegedly unleashes, (2) the services chapter, and (3) the provisions related to subsidies. We have already dealt with the harmonization issue in the previous section. Let us instead focus on points (2) and (3).

The FTA's implications have been the cause of much concern among groups involved with broadly defined social services. These groups maintain that the Canadian social fabric is very different from that of the United States, and that the FTA threatens to force the elimination of these differences. This subtle argument relies not on the harmonization thrust, but instead on the back-door or loopholes that the FTA supposedly contains.

The FTA covers many services—called covered services—while exempting many others—called non-covered services.    For maximum exclusion, the FTA only lists covered services.  The key non-covered services that are exempted from the terms of the FTA (including the national treatment obligations) include transportation, basic telecommunications, medical, legal, and child care, and all government-provided health, education, and social services. What does this exemption for non-covered services mean in practice?  It means that the government can make any rules or regulations it wishes for such services as health care, it can apply these rules differently to Canadian and U.S.-owned firms, and it can nationalize or exclude U.S. operators altogether.

But, claim the critics, it is the inclusion of management services as a covered service that creates the back-door through which low U.S. standards will creep into Canada and erode its social welfare programs.   The inclusion of management services means that if a province decides, for example, to privatize the management of one of its social services, it must adhere to the principle of national treatment.   In effect, the Canadian province must allow U.S. firms opportunities equal to those given to their Canadian counterparts in supplying the service.   However, this is not in itself a sufficient condition to spell the end of high-quality Canadian social welfare programs.   Canadian governments could under these conditions still determine whether or not a management service is to be contracted out or kept in governmental control.   It also maintains power over the laws, rules, and regulations governing the provision of these services whether it is provided by a Canadian or U.S. national.   Furthermore, many social services are provided for through provincial procurement policies, which are, in any case, not under the obligations of the FTA.

The subsidy issue relates mainly to business subsidies in general, and to regional development subsidies in particular.   With the country divided into regions with varying levels of prosperity, Canada has relied to a great extent on regional development subsidies that have become a part of the social policy framework— just as equalization payments are a part of the Canadian constitution. Critics of the FTA maintain that because regional development subsidies were not given exemption from U.S. trade remedy laws, they are at risk from U.S. countervail. This is without doubt true, but it is not particularly revealing.  Although the FTA does not grant Canada an exemption from U.S. countervail, it does absolutely nothing to increase the risk of U.S. retaliation. The FTA does not limit the right of Canadian governments to use regional development subsidies to encourage economic growth. The FTA leaves these subsidies just as they were before the agreement was signed—at no more or no less risk than if the FTA had not been signed.

The FTA mandates negotiations to develop a bilateral set of trade remedies to replace the domestic application of these laws on both sides of the border. In the meantime, several temporary measures are in place. Specifically, the legislative watchdog to oversee any changes in either country's current trade laws, and a binational panel to replace judicial review in cases involving countervail and antidumping. In view of these provisions we do not concur with the critics' contention that Canadian subsidy policies are in jeopardy. It would be hard to imagine that U.S. attitudes toward Canadian regional subsidy practices would change in light of binational scrutiny and historical precedents.[4]

Even more disturbing to supporters of the FTA is that any reforms of social programs are being made increasingly difficult and highly politicized because they are being linked to the FTA by its opponents. This is unfortunate and misguided since the need for social policy reform in Canada is independent of the FTA. Canadian social programs have become burdensome to the public purse and have largely failed to achieve their stated objectives. For example, calls for unemployment insurance reform were heard as far back as 1984. In this case, Canada needs a system that facilitates and enhances labor-market adjustment, rather than impedes it like the current system. Seen in this light, if the FTA forces policymakers to reform Canada's social programs to make them more efficient and more effective, then it should be considered one of the FTA's benefits and not one of its perils.

## V. CULTURE

The debate over the "Canadian identity" and Canadian culture has been around since Canada was founded well over a century ago. On one side are those who believe the Canadian identity is weak and fragile and not strong enough to withstand more truck and trade with the Yankees. On the other side are those who believe that the Canadian identity is deeply entrenched and so trading a bit more with the U.S. will not make Canadians more like Americans.

4. This view is supported in Horlick et al. (1988).

### Canadians Are Not Americans

Canadians have always had a steady diet of U.S. arts and culture—books, newspapers, magazines, movies, and television.  But in our view, this has not meant that Canadians have or will become Americans, though many affinities are shared by the two peoples. The reason for our position lies in the belief that the Canadian cultural heritage is deeply rooted in history, political economy, geography, and immigrant experiences that are in contrast to those expressions of our neighbors to the south.   Differences in the cultural heritage of the two countries stem from the founding events that gave birth to each country.  The heritage of the United States lies in the American Revolution, while the heritage of Canada lies in counter-revolution and the absence of any war of independence.

There are deeply ingrained differences in the way the two countries govern themselves and view the role of the state.  The U.S. Constitution puts forth as paramount the rights of individuals in "life, liberty and the pursuit of happiness."  By contrast, Canada's governing document stresses "peace, order and good government," which suggests the importance of society over personal liberties. This has also meant that Canadians take a different view of government as a friend and partner.  Geographically, Canada is the second-largest nation in the world but is inhabited by a small population of only 25 million people.  Much of the country, however, is less hospitable than the smaller but much more hospitable United States.   This has meant that Canadians have come to rely much more heavily on direct government involvement in economic matters and social support.

The two countries have also had immigrant experiences that have contributed to their distinctiveness.   The influx of new people of many different ethnic backgrounds occurred much earlier in the United States than in Canada, and by much different people. According to sociologist Seymour Martin Lipset, this has resulted in the cultural "mosaic" in Canada as compared to the U.S. "melting pot."  Lipset contends that Canada is a society in which diverse ethnic groups are assured the right of cultural survival, while in the United States the desire is to incorporate diverse groups into one unified whole, which stems from the founding ideology of the American Revolution (Lipset 1989).

The Canadian separatist crisis a decade ago is one of the most striking examples of how different Canadians and Americans are. The election of a separatist government (the Parti Québécois) in Québec during the 1970s led to a crisis of national unity.  The way in which the crisis was resolved was distinctively Canadian. There was no civil war—no one took up arms when the Québec government raised the specter of splitting off from the rest of Canada. Instead, Canadians had a referendum—or at least the people of Québec did—to determine the outcome. This is unique given the history of other nations, which are often subject to political and military persecution in the face of a minority problem.

Some sociologists are critical of the "cultural approach" we have adopted here to highlight Canada-U.S. differences. These critics claim that differences in the two countries stem from differences in economic prosperity—Canadian culture lags behind U.S. culture because of differences in standard of living, which will be reduced as Canadian incomes move closer to U.S. levels. But this is not supported by empirical evidence. Over time, the Canadian standard of living has grown so that it is now more than 90 percent of the U.S. level in terms of purchasing power parity.

After two decades of studying Canada and the United States, Professor Lipset still maintains that significant differences remain (1989). In particular, he notes for example that:

1. Religious differences continue to exist;
2. the United States has grown to become more centralized politically, while Canada has moved in the opposite direction;
3. large differences in violent crimes still exist;
4. Canadian governments have become even more supportive of equalitarianism and an activist welfare state, while the United States has returned to advocacy of a weaker state, one less involved in redistributed welfare programs; and
5. a distinct English-speaking Canadian culture continues to exist.

### Cultural Policy and the FTA

The second level of objection from the cultural community comes from the presumption that the FTA fails to protect cultural policies from U.S. retaliation, and that the terms of the treaty will erode support for such programs. Are these claims valid?

The Canadian cultural community asked for and received complete exemption from the obligations of the FTA. However, in return for granting complete exemption for cultural industries, the United States preserved the right to seek compensation for discriminatory Canadian cultural policies. This clause (Article 2005.2) has created much concern and is worth quoting in full:

> Notwithstanding any other provision of this Agreement, a party may take measures of equivalent commercial effect in response to actions that would have been inconsistent with this Agreement but for paragraph 1 [which exempts the cultural industries].

Although some people worry that this clause places cultural policies in jeopardy, we do not share this concern. Consider the following points, drawn from Lipsey and York (1988, chap. 20):

1. Government support for cultural policies—subsidies to sports, music, ballet, and Canadian literature—which do not conflict with free trade remain unaffected.
2. The cultural exemption means that Canadian governments can discriminate between nationals of either country.
3. The United States has always had the right, under the GATT, to retaliate against discriminatory cultural policies. So the FTA seems to do no more harm than to formalize the status quo. In the past, the United States has used this right to retaliate against discriminating Canadian policies, such as Bill C-58.
4. The binational dispute settlement mechanisms contained in the treaty will ensure that any U.S. retaliation is at most "equivalent to commercial effect." This is an improvement over the previous situation, wherein unilateral U.S. retaliation could not be assessed.

The above suggests that Canada is free to follow any cultural policies it wishes at the cost of compensation to the United States if such policies are discriminatory in effect. This does not seem to us to be an unreasonable cost, and is one that Canada would have demanded if the United States asked for such an exemption with respect to some other industry. In the future, Canadian policymakers must ask themselves if the objectives and benefits of instituting some new discriminatory cultural policy is worth the possible cost of "equivalent-effect" U.S. retaliation.

## VI.  CONCLUSION

Canada and the United States are neighbors along the world's largest undefended border and partners in what has become the world's largest bilateral trade flow—US$168 billion worth of imports and exports annually. The FTA will further strengthen the long-standing friendship that these two nations enjoy.

From the Canadian point of view, the FTA is an important accomplishment. As a trading nation, Canada depends directly on exports for nearly 30 percent of its income—80 percent of those exports going directly to the United States. In our view, the best way for Canada to secure and enhance its cultural, social, and political independence is to secure and enhance its economic prosperity. The FTA is the means through which Canada-U.S. trade and investment will continue to grow, to the benefit of both countries' employment, incomes, and living standards. Thus, we do not see the Free Trade Agreement as spelling the end of "Canada as we know it," but rather as the means through which we can achieve a "Canada as we want it."

## REFERENCES

C.D. Howe Institute. 1986. *Policy Harmonization: The Effects of a Canadian-American Free Trade Area.* Toronto: C.D. Howe Institute.

Government of Canada. 1987. *Canada-U.S. Free Trade Agreement.* Ottawa: Department of External Affairs.

Helliwell, John F. 1989. "From Now Till Then: Globalization and Economic Cooperation." *Canadian Public Policy.* XV Supplement (February).

Horlick, Gary N., Debra Valentine, and Debra P. Steger. 1988. "Two Views on Dispute Settlement and Trade Laws in the Canada-U.S. Free Trade Agreement." *Trade Monitor,* no. 6. Toronto: C.D. Howe Institute.

Lipset, Seymour Martin. 1989 (forthcoming). *Distinctive Neighbors: The Values and Cultures of Canada and the United States.* Washington and Toronto: Canadian-American Committee.

Lipsey, Richard G. 1988. "Free-Trade Opposition Sprang from Well-Nurtured Ground." *Financial Post* (December 12).

Lipsey, Richard G., and Robert C. York. 1988. *Evaluating the Free Trade Deal: A Guided Tour Through the Canada-U.S. Agreement.* Toronto: C.D. Howe Institute.

# INDEX

# ABOUT THE CONTRIBUTORS

**William F. Averyt** is Associate Professor of Business Administration at the University of Vermont, where he serves on the Executive Committee of the Canadian Studies Program. In 1988, he received the Award for Excellence in Teaching and Service.

**Jean-Thomas Bernard** is Professor of Economics at Université Laval, where his work is in applied econometrics, natural resources economics, and industrial organization. He was a Research Fellow at Harvard University in 1987-1988.

**Peter Brimelow,** Senior Editor of *Forbes* magazine and columnist for the London *Times* and the Toronto *Financial Post,* is the author of *The Patriot Game: Canada and the Canadian Question Revisited* (Hoover Institution Press 1987/Key Porter 1986).

**Maureen A. Farrow** has recently rejoined The Coopers & Lybrand Consulting Group as Partner and Chief Economist following a two-year term as President of the C.D. Howe Institute. She serves on the Social Sciences and Research Council of Canada and is past president of the Canadian Association of Business Economists.

**Jane S. Little** is an Economist at the Federal Reserve Bank of Boston. She is a member of the Commonwealth of Massachusetts Committee on International Trade and Investment.

**William S. Merkin** served in the Office of the United States Trade Representative as Deputy Assistant U.S. Trade Representative for Canada and Deputy Chief U.S. Negotiator for the Canada-U.S. Free Trade Agreement negotiations. He resigned in January 1989 and is currently Senior Vice President of the International Division at Strategic Policy, Inc.

**Jack R. Miller** is Senior Partner at Fasken Martineau and Walker, advising clients on the Canada-United States Free Trade Agreement and on the GATT. He is currently the Québec Vice-Chairman of the Fasken Martineau Walker Trade Law Committee .

**Frank Stone** is Senior Research Associate at the International Economics Program of the Institute for Research on Public Policy in Ottawa, with a special interest in Canadian and international trade policy.

**Robert C. York** is Policy Analyst at the C.D. Howe Institute, and Canadian Research Director for the Canadian-American Committee. He is the author of numerous studies on Canadian trade policy, including *Evaluating the Free Trade Deal: A Guided Tour through the Canada-U.S. Agreement* (1988) with Professor Richard G. Lipsey.

# ABOUT THE EDITOR

Daniel E. Nolle is Assistant Professor of Economics at Middlebury College. He has published articles on U.S.-Japan trade and on intra-industry trade. His current research focuses on industrial organization and international trade. Prior to joining the Middlebury College faculty in 1987, he was an Economist at the Federal Reserve Bank of New York. He worked in both the Foreign Exchange Department and the International Research Department, where he prepared the U.S. current account forecast and engaged in research on U.S. foreign direct investment, as well as the macroeconomic and trade policies of the major industrial economies, with an emphasis on Canada and Japan.

Professor Nolle obtained his Ph.D. from Johns Hopkins University.